*Practicing
the Prayer
of Presence*

Practicing the Prayer of Presence

ADRIAN VAN KAAM

and

SUSAN ANNETTE MUTO

Resurrection Press
Mineola • New York

Imprimi Potest: Rev. William R. Headley, C.S.Sp.

Nihil Obstat: Rev. William J. Winter, S.T.D.
            Censor Librorum

Imprimatur: Most Rev. Vincent M. Leonard, D.D.
            Bishop of Pittsburgh
            February 28, 1980

Revised Edition published in 1993 by
            Resurrection Press, Ltd.
            P.O. Box 248
            Williston Park, NY 11596

ISBN 1-878718-14-2

Library of Congress Catalog Card Number 91-83751

Cover photograph and design by John Murello

Printed in the United States of America

Contents

Preface ix

Foreword xvii

BOOK ONE
Practicing the Presence of God

1   Our Need for Contemplative Presence 5

2   Presence in the Life of a Christian 19

3   Differences between Secular Meditation
     and Christian Prayer of Presence 35

4   Practicing the Presence of God 47

5   Silence and Presence 59

6   Obstacles to Growth in Prayerful Presence 70

7   Creating Conditions for Growth in Presence
     to the Divine Presence 83

8   Coming Closer to God 103

BOOK TWO
Prayers of Presence

PART ONE: PRAYERS BY ADRIAN VAN KAAM 111

Icon of the Living God 112
Witness for Your Light 113
A Living Message of Gentle Love 114
Fleeting Sense of Your Abiding 115
The Woman at the Well 116
Song for God 117
Trusting in Your Presence 118
The Everlasting One in Whom We Share 120
If We Would Only Know 121
Staying with Grace 122
Fill My Emptiness with Longing 123
Mystery of Living Water 124
Create a New Heart in Me 125
The Winter of My Heart 126
You Read My Heart 127
Useless Servant 128
You Stand at the Door and Knock 130
We Believe in You 131
Let Me Move in Your Presence 132
Lord, Rescue Us 133
With a Contrite Heart 135
Gentle Vision 136
In Your Sight 137
Lovely Spirit of The Lord 138
Let No Anger Grow in Me 139
Let Me Not Silence My Aliveness 140
Land of Love 141
Praise to You, Lord Jesus 142
Tender Flower of Holy Presence 143
Present to My Daily Task 144

Let Me Dwell Daily in Your Love 146
The Mystery of Your Will 147

PART TWO: PRAYERS BY SUSAN MUTO 149

The Prayer of Inner Quiet 150
The Peace You Promise 152
Your Own Presence in Me 153
Mist Shrouds Your Mystery 154
Without You, I Accomplish Nothing 155
The Grace of Sharing 156
Pilgrim at Your Door 157
You Listen to Love 158
To Wait Upon Your Word 159
We Love Your Name 160
To Wait Upon Your Will 161
To Soar Homeward with Ease 162
A Channel of Your Mercy 163
Why Do I Doubt Your Presence 164
Turn My Steps toward Home 165
Yes to the Father 166

Preface

This book opens us to the peace and purpose of living a life of Christian prayer. It teaches us how to pray and especially how to appreciate and practice the prayer of presence.

Before we delve more deeply into the style and rewards of this kind of prayer, we want to offer a few thoughts on the kinds of prayer people may offer to the Most High. Everyone can pray. Everyone can learn to pray, even to pray always.

We must understand prayer in the widest sense. To say prayers is one thing, whereas to live prayerfully involves a lifetime of growing, as did the Lord, in age and grace and wisdom before the Father (cf. Lk. 2:52). How does this inner unfolding take place? It can only occur when we are in tune with the inspiration and action of the Holy Spirit in our human spirit. This means being open to divine directives in the midst of daily life. Do we pay attention to the subtle movements of the Spirit in our ordinary lives? These directives are seldom overwhelming. Most often they are quiet whispers (invitations, challenges, appeals) to respond in a more Christlike way to other people, to events and things.

To live prayerfully necessitates that we seek to uncover the deeper meaning of life. To do so we have to learn to live reflectively, in a meditative way, rather than compulsively, in a superficial manner that hungers after every passing fad. As transcendent selves, we aspire to go beyond what statistics can measure and to open ourselves to the depth dimension of reality, even though this option entails suffering. Did not the prayer life of Christ lead to the cross?

Prayer is also a way to live as a unique, unified person in presence to the Divine Presence. One way to enter into God's presence is to take a single text from the scriptures or another inspiring text and enter into the meaning of the words in the light of our life experience.

Because we are made in the image and form of God, we must find ways of integrating the mystery with our day-to-day social world and our immediate situation as teacher, nurse, secretary, sales clerk, poet, doctor, lawyer, laborer. Prayerfully abiding with the text welcomes God into every corner of our daily life. It creates dispositions that open us to the sacred ground of reality from whence emerges our personal formation history.

This prayer of trustful presence is not meant to produce a spiritual high. It arises from that silence in which our heart hears the Lord's voice telling us of his love and assuring us that we need not be afraid. We know in the midst of doubt and suffering there is Someone upon whom we can rely. We resonate with the conviction that no matter what happens we cannot stop God from loving us. We may forget him, but he never forgets us. Each moment he calls us into being by that forming love that manifests itself not in fiery displays but in the ordinariness of the everyday.

Intercessory prayer, or prayer of petition, ought to be a frequent part of our life, especially when we bring before the Lord the needs of family members, friends, colleagues and students. In prayers of intercession we unite our will to God's. In faith and trust we ask humbly for all that we need. This prayer is impossible without faith, for it begins where reason and natural means to accomplish human ends cease to be effective.

When all human means are exhausted, when we witness the futility of our own efforts, we turn to God for mercy, for healing, for the fulfillment of physical and spiritual needs. This prayer acknowledges what we often feel: that God alone can satisfy our heart's desire. It is when we are powerless, vulnerable and out of control that God can work most freely in our lives. We allow God to be God because we have been reduced to nothing. Sometimes this prayer is composed of only one word: Help! We pray full of confidence that God always responds to human desperation. He does not scorn the broken, humbled heart (Ps. 51:17).

It may come as no surprise to learn that at least one saint, Catherine of Siena, saw a connection between intercessory prayer and contemplation. Petition for her was a unitive way of prayer because it unites the soul with God in all things. It brings him into every event of daily life and thus increases our experience of his presence. In her *Dialogue*, St. Catherine records the Father's invitation that we never relax our desire to ask for his help. Our intercessory prayers serve as intermediaries between a sinful, forgetful world and a forgiving, merciful God. With every intercession we affirm the relationship of love between God and all people.

Another way of prayer recommended by St. Teresa of Avila is conversation with Christ. In her own experience, she found it most consoling to keep up a running, interior conversation with her Divine Friend.

This prayer brings with it a happy, childlike feeling of trust and companionship. We can talk to the Lord of our trials and small triumphs, of our failings and of our thanks for his forgiveness. We may find ourselves quite literally talking to him while cooking supper or driving to work, before a class or after an important meeting. We soon learn that we can call upon him at any moment and find him near. At times this conversational intimacy may give way to moments of adoring distance or quiet nearness. Words fail to contain our gratitude and so we worship in silence.

Conversations with the Lord cover a range of topics as wide as the joys and sorrows of daily living. There is really nothing we do or have done that cannot be brought before the Lord. He understands it all. He illumines our minds when they are in darkness. He moves our wills despite indecision, touches our hearts, and draws us toward loving action. In conversation we discover again and again that God is Father, Friend, Guide, Lover. He enjoys speaking with us as much as we enjoy talking to him.

In these exchanges, verbal or wordless, each of us in our uniqueness experiences the personal love of God and grows toward new heights of transcendent presence. We gain courage to bear with misunderstanding, with the overt or subtle ridicule of those who do not understand or respect who we are and what we are called to do. When anger or frustration seems to get the best of us and we have no one to talk to at that moment, we are never at a loss, for our Divine Friend is always ready to listen.

Prayer is this continual interaction between us and God. It is the room in our hearts where God dwells always, the inner house his spirit fills. At times we are explicitly present to him in a posture of worship; at other times we are too busy to do anything but implicitly recall his promise.

Prayer is like a reservoir of divine energy continually being refilled inside us so that we can share its power with others in the world. If this is true, then how do we move from merely saying prayers, to ourselves becoming living prayer? The answer may be clear if we look at Jesus' encounter with the Samaritan woman (cf. Jn. 4:4–42). He takes this woman, deformed as she is by selfish desires, and draws her forth to worship the Father in spirit and truth. In the course of their encounter, he leads her from doubt, to petitionary prayer, to pure adoration.

We learn from this story that prayer means being able to converse familiarly with God at all times. It is not only a matter of asking for what we need but of living always in an attitude of thankfulness. Because God holds us in being, we can behold him in prayer. We can talk with God, hand in hand, detached enough from selfish desires to sense his spirit everywhere. We see, as it were, the invisible order of reality behind the visible. Like the Samaritan woman, we are astonished by the truth that God has come down from the mountaintop into the marketplace to seek us, to forgive us, to embrace us.

Prayer understood in this light is not a complicated procedure. It is as simple as breathing, as wondering, as beholding the mystery that lovingly holds us. We can no more stand outside this all-embracing love than a fish can exist outside the sea.

Becoming prayerful persons means attuning ourselves to the symphony of formation enfolding and energizing us at all times. We meet God in a sunrise, a smiling face, an inspiring text. We detect in unexpected quarters, like a hospital bed, his providential care. We realize that the dross of human fallibility covers the gold of human dignity. That is why we sense the divine presence in an aging parent, a sick child, a crippled beggar — in all who are suffering, vulnerable, imperfect.

We pray alone, of course, but we also pray as members of a community of faith, of a Church with a rich heritage and tradition. Our small prayers are inserted into the great stream of the Judeo-Christian liturgy, psalms, and devotions. These common prayers complement our personal petitions and raise worship above subjective expression. In the hymnal, for example, we find a gamut of expressions and emotions summarizing how God's people cry out for help, give glory to his name, plea for Christian unity, celebrate his birth, crucifixion, and resurrection from the dead. We can also research forms of prayer and meditation that have led people of other faiths to foster presence to the Holy.

Prayer as a way of being expresses itself in many ways. It can be a cry arising from anguish and torment, from loneliness and desolation; a song of joy ringing out in a moment of jubilation; a wordless peace between friends; a plea or intercession; a silent exchange between lover and Beloved.

Prayer is many things, yet it is one. It is the soaring of the human spirit to meet and be with the Spirit of God. It is heart calling to Heart, the alone with the Alone, the finite before the Infinite, the temporal at home with the Eternal. In prayer our human misery finds solace and strength in God's mercy.

We become living prayer when prayer affects every act and decision of our life. The world for us is not a place where people fight for survival but a house of prayer. Praying is not an experience reserved for a holy elite, but a mode of physical, mental, and spiritual survival. The choice is ours: we can erect barriers between ourselves and God, close doors, mete out love in stingy dribbles, and reap the meager results; or we can love God with our whole heart, soul, mind, and strength, pray without ceasing, and become the fully alive people God wants us to be.

This experience of practicing the prayer of presence has an effect, as we shall see, on every level of our life. The book you are about to read is, therefore, really two books in one. In the first we discuss different aspects of the practice of this prayer; in the second we offer examples of actual prayers of presence in the form of several original poems. Woven throughout the text are quotes and prayers that may inspire you to commit yourself to a way of life, a way of prayer, that may prove to be as challenging as it is transforming.

Foreword

Moments of contemplation in their simplest form happen spontaneously. We all experience from time to time these interludes of contemplation. A person may pause from the exertion of physical labor or concentration. She is captivated momentarily by the beauty of nature. Woods, oceans, lakes, clouds, mountains, trees, lowlands, skies — he feels at one with them all.

> ... *For I have learned*
> *To look on nature, not as in the hour*
> *Of thoughtless youth; but hearing often times*
> *The still, sad music of humanity,*
> *Nor harsh nor grating, though of ample power*
> *To chasten and subdue. And I have felt*
> *A presence that disturbs me with the joy*
> *Of elevated thoughts; a sense sublime*
> *Of something far more deeply interfused,*
> *Whose dwelling is the light of setting suns,*
> *And the round ocean and the living air,*
> *And the blue sky and in the mind of man*
> *A motion and spirit, that impels*
> *All thinking things, all objects of all thought,*
> *And rolls through all things.*

> — WILLIAM WORDSWORTH
> (FROM "LINES COMPOSED A FEW MILES
> ABOVE TINTERN ABBEY," JULY 13, 1798)

Often this contemplation of nature deepens to become a religious experience: a being touched and quieted by the Mystery of all that is. Our mind is restored to serenity, our body to harmony. We resume our work in a rhythmical flow of contemplation and action.

People today have crammed their senses and minds with so many things to crave, think about and do that they have lost this natural rhythm of presence and praxis. Is it possible to regain it? Can our Christian formation help us? Many people in the past also wanted to extend these natural pauses. They even discovered ways to induce this state or prolong it. Some especially interested in the practice of contemplation created styles of monastic life and exercises conducive to fostering this kind of spiritual awareness.

The Church from earliest times has supported their efforts. As a result its teaching about prayer and contemplation is deep and rich. Christianity teaches that the grace of God in Christ can transform these human styles and exercises in a profound way. These practices facilitate openness to the Divine Object of contemplation, whose presence surpasses all natural benefits.

Christian contemplation does not disclaim the benefits of natural or methodical contemplation, but it does complement and correct these by the power of grace and the light of Revelation. Spiritual masters and directors in our tradition try to help people learn how to contemplate. Their advice is handed down from generation to generation and is conserved in the writings of the fathers, doctors and teachers of the Church. Many of these texts have been declared free of doctrinal error. This means that these masters did not write anything in contradiction with Revelation as safeguarded by the Magisterium. The specific instructions given in these texts in regard to the *practice* of contemplation are not all related directly to doctrine. They are thus open to revision. Yet innovations should not be made lightly. The respect of the Church for these masters should make us cautious in questioning their directives. Their instructions have survived because they have proven to be effective for generations of Christians.

Unlike masters of contemplation in the East, western masters were influenced by the critical rationality, the experiential precision, and the theological sophistication of the western mind. Their instructions stand up well under scientific inquiry. Above all they were blessed with an enlightened intuition of the work of grace. Other masters, similarly graced, confirmed their descriptions of these experiences and attested to the soundness of the resulting directives.

Provided we take this rich history into account, innovation is not excluded. We could, therefore, envisage innovations and additions in four areas:

First, we recall that the development of contemplative practices and life styles usually was bound to monastic or active religious communities marked by specific aims, styles, works, and cultures and by the personalities of their founders. Certain instructions may be more typical of the history and situation in which members of such groups found themselves than of the Christian message as such. A first innovation could be to establish what is *foundationally* helpful for any Christian who wants to develop the life of contemplation.

Second, the masters wrote mainly for people already advanced in the spiritual life and living in an atmosphere conducive to practicing the prayer of presence. Additional advice may be needed for beginners who live in the modern world.

Third, as soon as the practice of contemplation is fostered outside the boundaries of specific monastic or religious communities, one is faced with a greater variety of people. It is no longer a question of instructing small numbers of faithful living under special conditions. This makes it necessary to modify traditional practices to suit particular types of people and their needs.

Finally, present day scientific research into some of the observable effects of contemplative practices has made us aware of the desirable or undesirable side effects of certain methods. This insight may give rise to needed modifications. The development of simplified contemplative practices should combine the best of the tradition with the best of contemporary findings, without putting any obstacle in the path of grace. We believe that these practices can be faithful to the traditions of Christian contemplation while taking into account the findings of modern science.

When we look today at the mushrooming of publications about meditation, we are struck by their disagreement as to its meaning and methods. It may be helpful at the start to remind the reader what we understand by Christian contemplation or the prayer of presence.

The Christian prayer of presence as described in this book is a prayerful presence in Christ to the Divine Presence of the Holy Trinity. It is marked by a quieting of the functional intellect and vital life. It is acquired by certain means, under the assistance of ordinary grace, and it inspires a transformation of one's personality and environment.

This mode of Christian contemplation is to be distinguished from secular meditation, which is a type of recollection aimed at fostering certain benefits, such as the inner balance, health and effectiveness of the meditator. Meditation books, by and large, address themselves mainly to this secular type of meditation. The proliferation of such texts exemplifies, if nothing else, the need for contemplative presence — a topic to be considered in Chapter 1 of this book. In Chapter 2 we will describe more fully what characterizes the practice of presence in the life of a Christian. Chapter 3 will clarify further the difference between secular meditation and Christian prayer of presence. Presented in Chapter 4 will be an instance of the practice of presence in the life of an exemplary Christian, Brother Lawrence of the Resurrection. Chapter 5 opens us to the world of silence — so conducive for the stilling that readies us to receive the gift of God's presence. Subsequent Chapters (6 and 7) will deal respectively with obstacles that may hinder our growth in prayerful presence and loving service and with ways and means to facilitate this presence.

The Epilogue of Book One, entitled "Coming Closer to God," will lead the reader into Book Two. There, in answer to the requests of many readers, we are publishing prayers of presence from previously written sources, retitled and collected here for the first time. These sources include, by Adrian van Kaam, *Spirituality and the Gentle Life, Woman at the Well,* and *Looking for Jesus,* and, by Susan Muto, *Steps Along the Way* and *The Journey Homeward.*

We express in these pages heartfelt thanks to our colleagues and students at the Institute of Formative Spirituality, especially to fellow faculty member, Father Richard Byrne, O.C.S.O., who graciously helped to ready the original manuscript for publication.

Remain in Me

Thank you for staying with me, Lord Jesus. If I had to remain in you by my force alone, I would soon betray your presence. You tenderly implanted me into yourself through the mystery of Baptism. How often I broke my oneness with you and hindered its unfolding. But you constantly restored the loving union that was lost. You attracted me; you permeated me with the sweet scent of your presence. I beg you, Lord Jesus, let your silent presence in me be a power of self-formation.

I hear you whisper in my soul: Remain in me, then I will remain in you. Your loyalty to me, my Lord, can never be questioned. You are fidelity itself. You loved me and pruned me before I could love you. Your acceptance of me is not hemmed in by impossible conditions. You are all for me even when I am against you. You cherish me no matter how I feel or am. It is only I who can be unfaithful to you. Therefore you have to ask me: "Remain in me." You assure me once and for all: "Then I will remain in you."

How direct and simple is the promise of your presence. You don't tell me that it is anything out of the ordinary. It is not a question of elated experiences. They may or may not accompany your presence in me. Your presence is not only for people more exalted than I, people unusually graced and gifted. It is also for me, a simple believer in your daily love and care.

To remain in you is not a feat of feeling or perfection. To remain in you is to believe in you, to surrender to you in faith, hope, and love. When I ask to remain in you, I ask for a special dimension of the grace of faith, the dimension of faith that is fidelity. Please, Lord, let faith and fidelity abound in me; let them fill the empty spaces of my life.

*Practicing
the Prayer
of Presence*

BOOK ONE

Practicing the Presence of God

LOVING TRINITY

Loving Trinity,
In the mystery of your love
You granted us
The precious power of reflection
On the way to at oneness with you.
Make us reflect on our lives,
On people, events and things,
Meditatively, gently, healingly.
Grant us a reflective vision
That rescues the simplicity
Which things radiate
In the splendor of your presence
Do not allow us to center
On ourselves alone,
As if we were not held constantly
In your loving light.
Let no anxious self-reflection
Tighten our hearts,
Nor pained concern
About our petty progress.
Save us, Loving Trinity,
From the pitfalls
Of self-centered piety.
Make us attentive
To your call
Beyond reflection,
Beyond images, forms and thoughts
Into the stillness
Of a wordless presence.

CHAPTER 1

Our Need
for Contemplative Presence

Many people today seem to have lost their direction. They are no longer in touch with the wisdom of creation. They seek for something to hold on to: politics on the far left or the far right, new philosophies, occultism, drugs, erotic experiences, exotic entertainments. Educated to cleverness not wisdom, they seem to prefer glamour to substance, yet deep down they crave for some ultimate meaning in their lives.

In their search they may be led to Holy Scripture and the writings of the spiritual masters. These works open their yearning minds to dimensions of meaning neglected or repressed in their life thus far. Yet reading them without guidance may be misleading. Many spiritual masters wrote for hermits and mystics. They addressed monks and nuns in deserts, monasteries or convents. Their readers came from communities of believers saturated with faith in mystery. Compared with us, they had a significant headstart. The master could safely invite them to peaks of mysticism because they had a solid foundation in faith and ascetical living. The same cannot be said of most present day readers.

These books unsettle us with descriptions of the rough path mystics had to tread to scale dazzling heights. We might conclude from a hasty reading that *any* kind of contemplation must be closed off from ordinary people living in the confusion of modern society. Yet contemplation in its simple, natural forms is as open to us as a flower to the sun. The path to this practice is not difficult, provided we understand what we are doing and travel in the right direction.

Even a person who has not practiced simple contemplation before may experience to her surprise that listlessness, insomnia, fears, worries, confusions and nervous symptoms begin to melt away. This natural practice of openness to the Divine Presence offers one many benefits. Persons who practice this prayer report a new-found confidence, relaxation and enthusiasm. They detect a bounce in their step. They seem more secure in themselves and are able to get along better with families and colleagues. They are more effective and at ease in their daily task. They in no way repudiate the everyday world. If anything, they seem to support and live in it in a deeper, more efficient way.

Such reports break down our stereotype of the withdrawn contemplative. People who contemplate plunge into social life and human concerns. Their pauses of presence are not an escape from participation; they are moments of rejuvenation for better service.

The practice of presence must not be seen merely as a means to cope with problems, though in many instances the problems themselves disappear. Persons who pray contemplatively are usually healthy, happy, well-functioning people who want to increase their effectiveness while opening their hearts fully to intimacy with God. We often sense that we are not functioning as well as the Lord has enabled us to do. We feel guilty for using only a fraction of our spiritual powers. We are gripped by the nagging awareness that there must be more to life than the snail's pace we are accustomed to.

The depressing notion that spiritual life must be a burden has been imprinted on many of us. Some gloomy writing and preaching insist that our life on earth is doomed. The only remedy is "to offer it up" and resign ourselves to unhappiness in this "valley of tears." Once it is all over, we may get our reward in the hereafter. Joy and peace in this world are not part of the plan of salvation. Such sentiments deform the spirits of many people, who appear to be untouched by the Good News.

The purpose of God's creation and of Jesus' salvation is our happiness. The formative power of God within us urges us to form ourselves in his likeness. We are impelled by this Divine Form to seek wholeness and holiness of life. Peace-filled joy, the blessed life, is the birthright of the Christian.

God created life as a gift to be treasured, not as a test to be endured. We share the glory of the Risen Lord. Suffering is unavoidable, but it is not meant to overwhelm and depress us. If we accept it in Christ, it can become redemptive. It only defeats us when we are unable to see its meaning. As Christians, we believe that within us is the indwelling Spirit of God, the Holy Trinity, who will make us whole and raise us beyond our misery.

All of us experience these hidden longings for peace and wholeness. We want to feel integrated deep down despite surface fragmentation, to enjoy equanimity in the core of our being, not to be torn apart by the strug-

gles we are caught in daily, to comprehend in a relaxed
way the situation we are faced with, to intuit quietly
its deepest meaning. We want to be like Jesus, com-
passionate, generous, gentle, giving and receiving love
in a gracious way. We desire to discern and follow the
unique direction of our life and to see in what way this
mysterious orientation fits in with the overall divine direction of humanity and universe. We want above all
to live in harmony with people, events and things and
the God who lets them be.

The practice of presence can help to satisfy such
longings. These possibilities for graced formation are
already implanted in us by the Holy Spirit. The prayer
of presence is simply a way of bringing out what is already there, as a seed waiting for rain so it can sprout
in once arid soil.

This aridity comes from the feeling of abandonment.
People complain of being alienated, uncared for, out
of touch with the meaning of life. To solve this problem initially, they may focus on external symptoms of
abandonment. Individuals and groups try to remedy
poverty, reduce oppression, end wars, clear slums —
as if without these problems human society would be
paradise on earth, as if utopian schemes would cure
unhappiness once and for all.

Many have tried to dissolve their unhappiness by
institutional changes. They try to emancipate the poor
by elevating them to membership in middle class society. But in exchange for their abandoned bodies, they
are given the right to become abandoned souls. They
are well fed with packaged food, enclosed in suburban
houses, breathing polluted air, competing anxiously
with the rest of us for more material goods, trying to
climb the ladder of status and success. Their spirit be-

comes as lonely and abandoned as ours already was. The moral is social change does not guarantee personal change. Relief of bodily abandonment does not prevent abandonment of soul. Social reformers, who have not found their own peace, are poison for the poor. No high-sounding phraseology can hide this truth.

As never before, it is becoming obvious that the abandonment of modern man is not merely a bodily phenomenon to be dissolved by material solutions; it is an abandonment of soul. Despite affluence, social care, and freedom from want, the experience of abandonment persists. Paradoxically it is often most pervasive in affluent societies. No legislation, education, or government funding has been able to relieve it. The richer, more educated and successful a person is, the deeper this sense of abandonment may strike him at unexpected moments.

Any attempt to solve social symptoms while ignoring abandonment of soul is most naive. Yet even today many are inclined to equate bodily abandonment with abandonment of soul. It is one thing to apply patches to a wound and another to deal with the underlying sickness pervading both oppressors and oppressed. To heal this malaise, we have to rekindle the spiritual life of all members of society, for its problems are traceable ultimately to the individuals who make up that society.

Is there a sound and simple way to help people cope with the experience of abandonment? One way would be the practice of the prayer of presence, for it brings a person in touch with her spiritual center where divine powers of formation abide. The form of this prayer is so simple that anyone can learn to practice it. In the following chapter, the actual method will be presented, but first we want to go further into the need for contemplative presence in today's world.

Restoration of this practice can be seen as a providential response to the needs of our time. We could compare it to the planting of a tree which, when full grown, will cover its surroundings with branches, leaves and blossoms. In its shade the weary traveller finds rest: The prayer of presence is like a place of repose for the seeker wearily crossing the desert of consumerism, competition, and computerized living.

Dwell, for a moment, on the phrase, "Heaven and earth are full of Your glory." Let this text and the reflection it evokes tap into your experience of this whole magnificent, diversified world filled with the glory of God. The dance of atoms and molecules goes on always and thus the world is always changing. The change in ourselves, in our surroundings, in the universe is not chaotic but ordered, for it is filled with the glory of God. Creation is permeated by a divine order. The human nervous system may undergo many alterations, but it does not take over the task of the kidneys or liver. Rivers do not stay frozen when the sun beats upon them. Palm trees do not produce peaches. Creation is not a child of haphazard change. It is permeated by a caring presence, suffused with an order of unsurpassed refinement and precision. The glory of God's formative power is everywhere. As Jesus said, no bird falls from the sky without the Father's knowledge. His loving order stretches out to embrace even the smallest creatures. Einstein said that the basis of his scientific work was the conviction that the world is an ordered and comprehensible entity, not a thing of aimless change.

The glory of God filling heaven and earth makes everything alter and grow while providing elemental structure, order and direction. His glorious self-manifestation in creation gives rise to an infinite variety of forms and expressions. Each of us is called to unfold in light of this divine direction at work in our personal lives and everywhere in the universe. Each of us is called to be a unique manifestation of the glory of God, unique and yet in harmony with the overall divine direction of universe and history. His glory directs us toward the growth and wholeness of the life form he has destined for us from eternity.

Heaven and earth are full of his glory. It is present in all forms of life and matter, in sky and earth, in minerals and plants, in everything we touch or taste, in our brains and nervous systems, in our bloodstream and organs, in our spirit, mind and senses, in our doing and our dying. His glory permeates past, present and future. We are within his glorious Presence the way fish are in the ocean or birds in the sky. We can resist his Presence but we cannot escape it. To flow with it is to feel peaceful, joyous and effective. To fight it is to suffer disorder, alienation and abandonment.

When we are at odds with the divine direction that structures all change in and around us, we cannot deal wisely with opportunities for personal transformation. When we are in touch with the Presence at the heart of the universe, we can find the truth we seek. The stillness of his Presence underlies the uncreated and created formative power sources that play in the universe. This power gives rise to an astonishing variety of forms, ever changing, yet ever directed.

The play of formative and transformative power in the universe may seem at first glance to be capricious. When we look more closely, we see that forms always arise, disappear and reemerge in accordance with a mysterious lawfulness. No person, event or thing can escape these divine laws of formation. The Creator infused his formative power into the very fiber of creation. This divine direction can be described by scientists as the laws of nature. The scientist can also identify the forms that emerge as different constellations of atoms. He can analyze the particles of atoms as protons, neutrons, electrons. He can even detect particles that are not particles in the strict sense but energy waves. The various constellations taken on by these building blocks of nature represent ever new forms of life and matter. But what science can neither measure nor analyze is the all-permeating Source of this steady, lawful emergence of forms — the silent presence of the formative power that structures this emergence.

This primordial formative power of God is alive in creation. It contains all the possible forms God has willed from eternity to emerge and unfold. Each person is permeated by this divine formative power. Human beings are created as free persons. Hence we are free to flow with or refuse the unique formation meant for us from eternity. God has granted us the great and unmerited gift of freedom of spirit. He has made us in his image and likeness. This means that we can be present to his divine direction at the heart of creation and in our own hearts, provided we silence our busy minds and listen to his call. In stillness we become aware of the directive presence of the Divine Persons in our inmost selves. At such moments we may pass naturally into contemplation. A silent presence pervades our spirit. Agitation ceases to overpower our interiority. Our heart is still as a mountain lake without a ripple. Everything is mirrored in its crystal clarity. We see anew without distortion. We are freed at such interludes of contemplation from concepts and images. Functional projects, illusions, and defenses slip into the background. Our pride is no longer the measure of all things. The truth sets us free. The Really Real, not the isolated "I," is the center, the Still Point of the turning world.

When we allow this divine force free play in our interiority, we taste the clarity of mind and purity of heart God meant for us. The Divine Director works in our organism as well as in forests and mountains, in seas and skies. However, the Holy Spirit directs the baptized person in a special way through the gifts of understanding, counsel and wisdom. God grants us an undeserved addition to the innate direction of creation. He makes us aware of our possibilities for graced service of self and others in the Kingdom.

We need to tap into these Spirit-enlightened powers in our human spirit and in the created powers of our organism. One means to establish and maintain this contact is through the prayer of presence. This simple form of contemplation — while graced and elevated by the Holy Spirit — is based upon the natural dynamics of the human spirit as God created it. The practice of presence spontaneously takes into account the Creator's formation of our whole organism. It rejuvenates mind and body, functional strength and vitality; it increases clarity of thought, efficiency in action, and relaxed determination in light of the unique limits and potentials granted to us.

Overwhelming descriptions of extraordinary states of contemplation may have shrouded for us the practical wisdom of the prayer of presence. This prayer should no longer be a well-kept secret for a select few but a living heritage for all Christians since contemplation is meant to transform the quality of all our lives.

The expansion of peace and joy comes easily and naturally to anyone who regularly contemplates. Most people live, in Thoreau's words, "lives of quiet desperation." They are stunted as human beings. They suffer from mild or chronic fatigue, from frustration and fearfulness. They only *appear* normal, sociable, religious and successful. Many of them live grimly by the word of God but never savor its sweetness. The joy of the Resurrection is not the core experience of their faith. Others may neglect codes of discipline. They pursue madly the fleeting satisfactions and pleasures life can offer while diminishing their graced potential for true joy. They are like thirsty people trying to catch rain drops falling from the sky with outstretched tongues while passing by huge wells of sparkling water.

Profound peace cannot be achieved by a panicky chase after pleasure and success. It is a gift granted to those who abide in contemplation. In quieter times and surroundings, contemplative interludes were normal. People turned to contemplation when they felt like it. It was their respite from worrying, planning, organizing. It restored their spirit, mind and body to sanity.

Whole populations today have become functionalized. They have lost the art of contemplative respite. Lacking normal restoration by contemplation, they are affected by chronic symptoms such as tension headaches, vague discomforts, breathing difficulties, frequent colds and flus, anxiety, bouts of despondency, high blood pressure, sleeplessness, excessive drinking and smoking, troubles at home and at work. Missing inner peace, they cannot live the full potential of a risen life in the Lord. Often they are irritable and aggressive, even if they try to hide their irritation under an obliging smile. They feel angry with the world at large because of their own frustration. Often they are chronic complainers. They have to put the blame somewhere, though it hardly ever occurs to them that paralysis of their contemplative potency has cut off their opening to joy and the blessed life.

Peace of mind is the healthy and natural state God created humanity to enjoy. It is not unattainable. It is, on the contrary, a grace residing within us. As long as we remain overinvolved in functional concerns, we cannot become aware of this gift. Our restless pursuits drain us. We run madly in many directions. We want to be freed from the general malaise that troubles us, yet nothing seems to lessen the discontent felt by a majority of people. Disenchanted with life, they look for someone or something that can open the door to enduring peace.

People are suffering not only from vague aches and pains, but also from emotional and interpersonal problems. They are marked by a backlog of past stresses that have accumulated in their nervous systems and in the muscle tensions and postures of their bodies. These organic traces of former strain keep them tight and tense; they absorb their energies and inhibit their graced capacity for peace and joy.

Periods of contemplation enable the organism to dissolve these nervous and hormonal remnants of past traumas and sufferings. The subsequent reduction of debilitating symptoms enhances the person's capacity for the gracious and effective incarnation of Christ's love in their life and surroundings.

Technology enhances production. What is produced must be sold. The need for such products has to be created in people. The media consequently evoke in us almost insatiable desires for comfort, travel, exotic foods, clothes, cars, sports, hobbies, entertainment, movies, T.V., radio, furniture, cosmetics — commodities that people a century ago could not have dreamt of. Every person wants her share in the unprecedented goods produced as the fruit of science and technology. Leisure time is also on the increase. Yet in spite of all this comfort, and consumption, there is an increase in neurosis, psychosomatic symptoms, drug abuse and alcoholism. Employers complain of poor performance. A pervasive absence of meaning invades people's lives, followed by a frenzied pursuit of stimulation.

This multiplication of needs and desires, of things to be bought or done, has intensified anxiousness, discontent and frustration. No one seems to escape this sickness. The rise of tension parallels the rise of technology everywhere in the world. Can this problem be solved? The solution is not to do away with technology, for it too is a gift of God. He created the human potential to develop the technical knowledge that can help us to safeguard and use wisely the gifts of nature in loving cooperation with the wisdom of creation. Cooperation is possible, provided we do not let technique run wild. Its power is blind. Experimental science, technology, production, and consumption, if allowed to grow wildly, will destroy us in the end. If our planet is to survive, we, as a world population occupying Planet Earth, need to experience anew the wisdom of divine creation. We have to distance ourselves from the blind search for stimulation and satisfaction.

Moments of simple contemplation take us out of this whirlwind of consumption and production. They insert a peaceful space in our programmed lives. They restore the contemplative foundation in our human make-up.

Once restored and cultivated, the fruits of contemplation will be found in the midst of action. The tension mounting in our daily lives will be relieved.

Restoration of the contemplative dimension is more necessary now than ever before. To understand why, we need only to reflect for a moment on the changes the technical world has wrought. For example, today we have to assimilate, as rapidly as a blink of the eye, experience and information that were gathered in the past over centuries. Overstimulation by information forces our minds, bodies and senses to function beyond their capabilities. The speed of transportation, computerized processing of information, mass communication and production tend to put us in constant agitation. This accelerated rate of change, invading every aspect of life, leads to continuous mental and physical strain. Our minds and organisms cannot withstand these unrelenting pressures. Health and harmony break down under the excessive wear and tear of too much change too fast. Our biochemical and physiological reactions to these challenges exhaust our energies.

Again we see the need for moments of quiet contemplation that will grant our organism sufficient rest to restore depleted bodily resources and ready us to serve the Kingdom. The practice of contemplative presence is a proven way to diminish our increased susceptibility to the diseases and psychosomatic ailments which can and do decrease our social and apostolic effectiveness. Let us, therefore, take time to be present so that this practice can help to restore our personal and spiritual lives.

TIME TO BE PRESENT

Lord, let me find back
The lost treasure of time:
Time for gentle listening to a friend,
For sharing the play of a child,
For consoling a suffering person,
For thinking without strain,
For labor without pressure.
Time to delight in birds and flowers,
Blooming trees and lustrous green.
Time to enjoy music, friends, and meals,
Time to be silent and alone,
Time to be quietly at home,
Time to be present to Your mystery.
Free me from the tyranny
Of time urgency.
Let time not possess me
Neither the pressure of daily concerns.
Let me not cram every moment
With useful or exciting things
To do or say.
Let my life be a gentle preparation
For the pure and precious moments
Of listening to you
So that I may not drown
In the rushing waters
Of practical pursuits.

CHAPTER 2

Presence in the Life of a Christian

The practice of presence to the Divine in ourselves and in the world involves a silent abiding that will transform our lives. Being both calming and invigorating, this practice makes us ready to incarnate God's love in our personalities and life situations. The effects of this prayer are visible not only in especially graced persons but also in the lives and emotions of ordinary people.

If this gift of presence is given to us, we must flow with it humbly. We should create conditions that foster it more fully. For instance, we need to enkindle the right desire. We should not want this presence merely because we have heard that it helps people to feel healthier, more creative and relaxed. We should enjoy such benefits but desire them mainly because they help us to become better vehicles for God's love in this world. A self-centered purpose could lead to complacency and pride and thus remove us from the Divine Presence.

This practice thus facilitates first of all the gift of presence. In a secondary way it can heighten the effectiveness and attractiveness of our service in Jesus to suffering humanity. To show this connection concretely we need only refer to research done in medicine, psychology, and psychiatry. While no science can test the work of God in us, it can study changes in attitudes and behavior in the body and nervous system, that flow from our presence to him. The scientist can observe these effects, and he may even pinpoint some of their causes. What he cannot measure is their main source deep in the soul.

The prayer of presence is not meant to replace other kinds of prayer or spiritual exercises. Liturgical prayer, prayers of petition, devotions, spiritual reading, reflective meditation, examination of conscience — all have their place in our spiritual life. This practice does not replace them; it is their partner. Its effects carry over and deepen our involvement in other kinds of prayer and spiritual exercises.

There are various ways of fostering this practice of presence to God. We will describe some of them, with the clear understanding that there is no one "right" approach. Each person should find the way congenial to him or her. We may try out different ways and then choose the one that proves to be most helpful. We may also want to use different approaches at different times. The Holy Spirit calls each of us to a unique way of presence. No matter what style we choose, the Spirit will color it in subtle ways. These nuances will be in tune with the unique way in which he calls us to live the life of Jesus. We will thus grow in a style of presence truly our own.

Simplicity of the Prayer of Presence

The prayer of presence is at once simple and spontaneous, elemental and profound. It affects in a positive way those who practice it, for example, by making them calmer even under adverse conditions.

The practice of presence is only one of many exercises handed down to us by spiritual traditions. It is, however, uniquely helpful because of its simplicity, spontaneity, effectiveness, and universality. It is compatible with all cultures and backgrounds; it enhances the spiritual exercises found in each of them.

The universal effectiveness of this prayer should not be surprising, for it deals with the deepest dimension of our life: the human spirit. When the human spirit is not fully developed and enlightened by the Holy Spirit, problems emerge on many levels. The human mind-unenlightened by the Spirit — becomes a breeding ground of negativity, frantic competition and comparison, of frustration and hostility, of anxiety, envy and distrust. These negative attitudes lead to defensiveness and aggression. They give rise to a world where the love of God is obscured.

The prayer of presence dissolves confusion and disorderliness; it sets creativity free. Through this prayer the Holy Spirit can help us to actualize the new creation in Christ that we already are. He may use this prayer to restore us to compassion and joy, to the quietly dedicated, innovative and effective service of a person filled with delight for God, himself, and others. Out of such gifts the Kingdom of God is built in the world as a pointer to the Kingdom that is to come.

The prayer of presence can thus lead us to inner peace and tension-free vitality. It can grant us a new zest for living. It is the door to a more rewarding experience of religion. It enables us to find the divine answer to our deepest longing for happiness, which God himself planted in the human heart.

The Healing Power of the Prayer of Presence

The prayer of presence is not a magical solution for all problems. Experience teaches us that it can be added to whatever else is going on in our spiritual life, usually with great benefit. This style of presence enables us to go beyond self-scrutiny or preoccupation with sin and imperfection, beyond anxious analysis of emotional problems. We become more able to share in the glory of the Risen Lord and hence to engage in daily activities with a joyful heart.

There are many stresses in life that interfere with our capacity for joy. The prayer of presence is one way of coping with patterns of deformative distress typical of the human condition after the Fall. Our self-preoccupation, the belief that we have to be our own saviors, may block our ability to relax and enjoy ourselves as children of God's Kingdom. Even when threats are absent we may dream them up. We seek relief from such stresses in tranquilizers and therapies. These may be helpful in some cases, but their effectiveness is limited. A person may gradually replace them by the practice of presence if approved of by the physician or therapist treating her. In fact a number of doctors have found that people who suffered from nervous tension did benefit from this practice.

How is this possible? Can our body in any way profit from something as spiritual as prayer? Can the gift of peace that the Holy Spirit grants have a calming influence on our nervous system?

We are so accustomed to thinking of our bodies as separated from our spirit that we are surprised to hear the suggestion that there may be some connection. And indeed there is. The practice of presence may lead to moments of peace. This peace of the Spirit does not necessarily stay enclosed in our soul. Our soul is not a separate compartment with no opening whatsoever to our bodily life. Peace of soul may have a quieting impact on brain and nervous system. This effect can be studied. As a matter of fact it has been investigated by scientists. They found to their surprise brain wave changes in persons during contemplation. These changes were typical of people whose nervous system and organism had calmed down considerably.

When we quiet down in this way, we become more joyous and lighthearted. These bodily effects are only passing signs of a far deeper change in our soul that cannot be observed or measured. The impact of grace in the core of our life is invisible. It may spill over, however, into our organism, extending the joy and peace already effected by these quieting practices.

We may ask ourselves if this calming of our nervous system has any meaning for our daily life in Christ? This quieting may diminish symptoms of tension such as irritation, nervous twitches, angry outbursts. Such symptoms do not affect our inner graced life before God. What these defects may mar is the witness value of our Christian life. It may be difficult for others to see in our daily comportment the invisible peace and joy God grants us inwardly. In other words, such nervous symptoms may hinder the easy outflow of our inner love and peace into public life. We may be less attractive an incarnation of divine care and compassion in this world.

Even if we do not suffer such symptoms, the prayer of presence may have an impact on our apostolic life. It will neutralize daily deformative stresses and prevent the development of symptoms that would make our apostolic presence to others less appealing and effective.

It is true that the practice of presence may alleviate painful consequences of deformative stress in our lives. This does not mean that God will take all suffering away. Suffering will remain suffering, but God's grace may relieve the impact of suffering on our life. He may turn deformative into formative stress. That is a far more long-ranging effect than the relief of organic symptoms. This grace of inner resilience will enable us to maintain equanimity in the deepest recesses of our life. The more we follow this practice, the more the Lord will enable us to keep our balance, even under unusual stress. God may help us also to regain in a shorter time the peace we lose when the burdens of life become too much to bear. He may let us realize at such moments that life since the Resurrection is meant to be a participation in the strength and peace of the Risen Lord.

We suffer because of limits imposed on our life while our spirit aspires to live without limits. Hence, frustration abounds when we hurl ourselves against the boundaries of daily existence. The prayer of presence makes us one with the unlimited inspirited life within and without us. We become present in faith to the boundless beauty of Jesus Christ. In the light of this faith, we are less overcome by the limitations of everydayness. We perceive our limits as permeable lines of demarcation not as barriers to union with the Divine. Our life begins to participate in the Risen Life of Christ. This quality of life is radiated to others and effects some change in the atmosphere around us.

We become like the salt of the earth, the light on the mountain. If we become better Christians, society will become better. Gaining peace-filled joy, we will help to change the trends in society from strife and tension to peace and cooperation. This increase in mutual care and love marks the dawn of the Kingdom — the coming of a better world, envisaged by Jesus and proclaimed by his disciples.

Progress has been difficult for humanity. Human nature, as God created it, was meant to enjoy a wisdom and balance that kept it in tune with the divine direction of the universe. The Fall distorted this balance and obscured this wisdom. Since the Fall we live in a troubled world. We are inheritors of a confused humanity. But in Jesus we are called by the Spirit to change the world. It may still be dark for us but Jesus inaugurated the dawn of a new day.

The human spirit before the Fall was not out of tune with the wisdom of God as it manifested itself in the rest of nature. God filled the universe with a silent direction. He infused his creative wisdom in his creatures and in the mysterious laws of their unfolding. The human spirit had no difficulty to move, act and unfold in harmony with this divine direction of cosmos and other creatures. Since the Fall, we seem to be out of tune with the wisdom of the divine image or form embedded in our nature. Jesus restored this balance when he assumed our nature and enabled us to regain the possibility for obedience to the divine direction.

The practice of presence lifts the veil that hides our

nearness to God. We begin to see and act in harmony with the image and form in which we are created. We make fewer mistakes in the art of living. The mistakes that result from our fallen nature are a source of unhappiness. When our human presence is enlightened by the presence of the Holy Spirit, the results are life-enhancing. We begin to flow with the sacred source of nature. If we are driven only by our need to use nature, we cease to enjoy the beauty of trees, flowers, animals and people as expressions of the Unspeakable who fills the universe with his glory. The practice of presence restores this ability. As a result we begin to use nature more carefully and wisely, less greedily. We are not as easily inclined to destroy or pollute our surroundings and therewith to destroy ourselves. We listen to what God meant to tell us in and through the nature he created in and around us. This is part of what Jesus describes as obedience or doing the will of the Father.

Obedience comes from the Latin word *obaudire* meaning attentive listening. The attitude of obedience is at the heart of the practice of presence. Jesus is our example of this listening presence. Being obedient, doing the will of the Father, was the central meaning of his life. Jesus not only restores our obedience to the Father as he speaks in creation. He also gives us the Holy Spirit. The Paraclete is at the heart of our restored humanity. Through him we have access to a double source of wisdom: the divine direction of creation as a whole and the personal direction of each creature by the Father's will. The prayer of presence keeps us in touch with both of these sources.

The vision of the new age, the Kingdom Jesus speaks about, is not a fanciful dream. We believe in it because it is grounded in Revelation. The Spirit harmonizes us inwardly with our own nature and outwardly with all creation as a gift carrying the eternal wisdom of God. The life of faith does not make us floating, unrealistic, secluded from the world of everydayness. The more we live the practice of presence, the more straightforward, natural, and down to earth we become in what we see, say and do.

By contrast, since the Fall, we tend to be over-involved in a man-made world we have superimposed on creation. Not all aspects of this world of ours are a witness to the harmonious unfolding of the divine wisdom alive in the universe. Some of these inventions are like a counter-creation, as is clear from reflections on air and water pollution, on drug and alcohol abuse, and, on the utilitarianism of our educational systems.

If we get involved too excitedly in our functional projects, it is hard for us to listen to God's presence and direction. The practice of presence calms this frenzy. It helps us attain an inner state in which we are not unduly agitated by our projects, passions, worries and perceptions. In this state of inner calm, we begin to intuit God's presence in grace and nature. We flow quietly with our own life direction within the overall graced direction of the universe. It is not a direction we grasp in clear and distinct concepts. Its communication is so subtle that we may not know where we are going when we listen. Yet this silent divine communication exercises its power in our life, guiding us in such a way that we find ourselves thinking, feeling, perceiving, and acting more in tune with our divine destiny in history and humanity. Because we are in touch with who we most deeply are, we avoid the problems that arise out of dissonance with the directions of life. We are put back on the road of our divine life formation.

Even if only a small number of Christians attain this restoration, their impact on society can be surprisingly great. We have only to remember the images used by the Lord to illustrate this truth. He compares true believers to the light on the mountain, the leaven in the dough, the salt of the earth. Only a little salt is necessary to make large dishes tasty. A small number of Christians in touch with the Spirit can restore hope in humanity and make life meaningful again.

When we fly at night over a mountainous region, we can see specks of light on the dark peaks reaching out to us. They are few in number yet they suffice to guide numerous planes to a safe landing. They create order in flight patterns, prevent collisions, and direct the movements of pilots high in the sky. People present to the Lord also radiate like specks of light their inner harmony with grace and nature. Their presence awakens people around them to their own divine direction. Like the leaven in the dough, they vitalize humanity and enkindle hope in countless people.

The Christian Practice of Presence

What does this practice entail for the Christian? The standard time-tested answer is that at least once a day for fifteen minutes to half an hour we recollect ourselves before God. We draw gently away from our daily concerns and activities, close our eyes or look quietly at a crucifix, the tabernacle, a statue or painting. We may gently allow a meaningful word from scripture, liturgy, a spiritual master, or a text of our own choosing to surface in our mind. We may also remember a religious symbol that has been inspiring to us. In and through the repetition of that look or that word or that remembrance, we become more present to the Presence within, to that mysterious life that is already ours as baptized Christians. Preferably we try to repeat this prayer of presence once or twice during the day at wisely spaced moments.

The Christian who is faithful to this practice can inspire other men and women of good will. Through his or her presence shines the glory of God's goodness.

The prayer of presence clearly does more for the Christian than grant the benefits of improved health and thought patterns that can be measured by science. Though valuable in their own right, and also a gift of God, these benefits are not the end of this prayer. It is above all a practice that helps us to discover a divine peace and joy; it is a sharing in the present glory of the Risen Lord. His Resurrection restored humanity's possibility for attaining the blessedness we all seek. No longing is more deeply implanted by God in the human heart, yet many experience life as a burden. They feel that equanimity is almost impossible to maintain, that it demands excessive effort. Sadly, many people complain about disquiet and disappointment. Disillusion seems so common, fulfillment so rare. The prayer of presence can reverse this imbalance. It is one of the means that the Spirit can use to help us discover our potential for graced and gracious living, no matter what circumstances we find ourselves in.

Since the Resurrection, life should not be filled with anxiety. It does not have to be merely a burden. When we share in the presence of the Risen Jesus, peace does not have to be a fleeting experience. It can be steadily expanded and deepened.

Almost everyone faithful to this prayer can discover that wholeness is not a feeling anxiously sought for or vaguely remembered; it can become an everyday experience. The peace of living in Christ's presence is neither a rare reward nor an idle illusion; it is the birthright of any person baptized in the Lord.

Caution Regarding the Therapeutic Value of this Prayer

The prayer of presence is not therapy. The Christian in treatment for any problem should keep consulting her physician or psychotherapist. The graced practice of contemplation leads to union with God, but it is not a panacea. It does not cure magically nor does it solve instantly a lifetime's accumulation of tension. It is certainly not sufficient to heal people severely disturbed or suffering from chronic ailments. They need treatment in addition to this practice. They should not discontinue medication prescribed for them without permission of their physician, no matter how well they may feel as a result of this practice. Regular contemplation may enable people to reduce certain kinds of medications, such as sleeping pills and tranquilizers. If they are prescribed, however, one ought to discontinue or reduce them only in consultation with his physician.

The prayer of presence is thus much more than a way to relax, calm down, throw off the pressures of everyday life. It may also have these effects. Yet it is first and foremost a way to develop one's graced potential for communion with God.

Service and Contemplative Presence

Awareness of the Divine Presence can be practiced anywhere — in planes, trains, buses, in offices and

waiting rooms, between classes, conferences, and appointments. These in-between moments enable us to
maintain this presence all during the day. They relieve
strain and restore our remembrance of God. This is not
to equate labor with contemplation. When engaged in
our work, contemplative presence necessarily recedes
in the background of our attention. In the foreground
is our presence to the task at hand. We are speaking
here about those "empty" moments *in-between* different
tasks.

During these moments our contemplative presence
can again come to the fore. This remembrance re-
news our conscious union with the Lord and lessens
unnecessary tension. Strain accumulates during our
working hours. As the day grinds on, we become less
efficient, prudent, and alert. Stress often becomes distress. Energetic participation in social and professional
life produces reactions in our muscular and hormonal
systems. Such reactions keep us productive. When excessive, however, they can become counter-productive.
For example, a middle-aged person who shovels snow
too fast and vigorously may end up with a stroke. An
overexcited messenger of the Good News may trip over
his words and repel his listeners by a careless approach
to the Gospel message.

Any arousal affects our organism in the same way. It
does not matter if the arousal is due to pleasant or un-
pleasant experiences. A person with a heart condition
may have an attack when he hears he has won the mil-
lion dollar lottery. Whether we are excited by anger or
passionate love, by failure or success, by frustration or
enthusiasm, by opposition or victorious determination,
by a moving community experience or a boring routine,
our nervous and hormonal reactions are set in motion.

The practice of presence in-between our workaday demands will mitigate the impact of such experiences. In contemplative presence we move away from absorption in the demands of daily life. This in-between prayer brings us back to the still point of our soul. Renewal of presence creates distance between us and what troubles or excites us during working hours.

As Christians we must not refrain from service, from participation in our culture, from the battle for peace and justice. But in the midst of service, of cultural creation and invention, we can restore the freedom of non-attachment. Stress is an invigorating ingredient of life; it does not have to become deformative distress with its crippling effects.

The prayer of presence keeps us relaxed and gracious in the face of opposition. We want to be kind and patient with people, but we become irritable because of the tensions that accumulate in us during our ministry. We become tense and tired under the constant demands made upon us. We lose our patience. Those around us experience that loss as a threat or disappointment. They become edgy in turn. Their words and conduct become defensive or aggressive. Our tension mounts; it increases theirs in turn, and so on.

The prayer of presence lifts us to a transcendent level where excitement and the pursuit of success have less of a hold upon us. We regain our composure and become able again to be lovable and useful to others as Jesus was. The practice of presence should not turn into a self-gratifying exercise that makes us oblivious to the needs of our neighbor. The true Christian turns any inspiration to the greatest advantage for society within the limits of her possibilities and his calling. The prayer of presence enables us to unfold to the full our capacities for incarnation. This practice unlocks for us the possibility of living a meaningful life within the Eternal Word through whom all things came to be and in whom all things are sustained in loving affirmation.

HELP ME TO BE PRESENT

Thank you, Lord, for choosing to live most of your life the routine of everyday labor. You have given me an example of the way in which I can sanctify myself in the quiet of a day-to-day spiritual life lived within the limits of an unpretentious situation.

I know, my Lord, that countless works can be done for you. But out of all these works, you in your love want only certain works to be done by me. You alone know the works that will be mine You reveal these works to me step by step. I cannot know, as you, how each work is linked to the work before and to the works you will ask me to do hereafter.

Sometimes I lose my path, but you always wait for me with infinite patience. You are the shepherd who returns me steadily to the pasture of my own work. Help me to be present in the simplicity of my heart to each work along the way you have laid out for me.

CHAPTER 3

Differences between Secular Meditation and Christian Prayer of Presence

Certain preliminary steps ready us for the prayer of presence, for example, quieting of the mind by repetition of a symbolic word. This preparation opens us to whatever initiative God may take in the depth of our self. Scientists who research the effects of quieting on human interiority have shown that even when such exercises are cut off from their traditional religious aim of union with God, the consequences are remarkable. These exercises enhance human health and productivity. Many psychiatrists, psychologists and medical doctors, representing various organizations and institutes, recommend these preparatory exercises as a means to aid health maintenance and prevent illness. They use various terms to define this process: centering or stress-reducing exercises, autogenic relaxation, practical meditation. The good results attained by people sometimes hide the fact that this preparation is at most a prelude to the prayer of presence. However beneficial its effects may be, the Christian cannot stop there.

Secular meditation can deepen self-awareness, effect a relaxation response, improve our physical condition. These benefits from the point of view of preparing for the prayer of presence may be excellent. The Holy Spirit may use this readiness factor to form our spirits in the image and likeness of Christ, to fill us with the joy and peace of the Risen Lord. In Jesus we become present to the Father in a way that is wordless and truly contemplative. However, secular meditation, pursued as an end in itself, leads in the long run to dissatisfaction.

The secular meditator may become aware of his aspiration for presence to a Divine Thou in faith, hope and love. Aspirations, however, which remain unfulfilled are more difficult to live with once they become conscious than when they were unnoticed. The awakening of the transcendent aspiration to encounter God explains why many people who start out doing secular meditation feel drawn after some time to return to or begin the prayer of presence. Guidelines for this prayer are given in the Christian formation tradition, but many of us have either neglected them or never explored their deepest spiritual meaning.

This return is by no means certain, for doing secular meditation can also lead to complacency. The meditator may feel satisfied with the limited effects this kind of meditation produces. She may regard her formation tradition as only a set of formulas, a list of do's and don'ts. Not suspecting its hidden promise, she prefers secular meditation because it means more in her life than her religion ever did.

In the Christian practice of presence, the person is receptive to the Holy Spirit as manifesting himself in a scriptural word or other symbol. He is present to the mystery of God's Presence. She allows the Spirit to transform her humanity. He recognizes that the mystery of God's Presence in Jesus is the response he is seeking to his deepest longings. This aspiration for oneness with the Divine is elevated by the Spirit, who deepens human faith, hope and love by infused faith, hope and love.

Our innate aspiration for presence to the Divine is confirmed in the humanity of Jesus. In him the prayer of presence reached its highest expression. As a Christian I share in Jesus' profound prayer — the prayer that enabled him in the end to surrender himself totally into the hands of the Father. The Christian practice of the prayer of presence is thus different from secular meditation. This difference affects the way in which the Christian goes about the preparatory phase of recollection or quieting. The secular meditator may mistake this preparatory phase for the prayer of presence itself. She may be animated by a mentality that aims at self-improvement and not at presence to the God of Revelation, whereas the opposite is true for the Christian.

We should be grateful that scientists continue to study the preparatory phase and its effects, but we should not see this phase in isolation from the full meaning of our prayer. These scientific results may help us in our own preparation. They may lead to an appreciation of how grace takes into account the vital and psychological structures of human formation. But we should make sure that the studies we consult are factual and that we do not follow indiscriminately certain merely secular views of life they may be built upon. We should also complement such studies with the revealed teachings of our Christian formation tradition. Only in this frame of reference do these research results find a

rightful place in the life of the person who aspires with
God's grace after Christian presence.

Recollection, Meditation, and Prayer of Presence

It is unfortunate that the preliminary steps to the prayer
of presence have been called meditation by secular and
westernized Eastern schools of meditation. In the Christian tradition of spirituality such steps are called neither
presence nor meditation. They are identified as recollection or inner quieting. The word "recollection" is a
combination of two words: to *collect*, which means to
gather, draw or bring together, and *re*, which means
again. To recollect is thus to draw together again. The
power of our spirit is invested in and spread out over
many attitudes and activities that preoccupy us during
any normal working day. It is necessary to bring our
spirit together again in inner stillness if we want to be
fully present to the Lord.

Recollection exercises are meant to re-gather this
scattered power of presence. If these exercises succeed,
energy output is withdrawn from our vital strivings,
probing minds, and functional performance. As a result, we experience rest and relaxation in both mind
and body. This quieting of our senses, brain and nervous system has an important side effect. The organism
can move from the outer-directedness typical of activity
to the inner-directedness typical of presence.

Recollection is not the same as meditation in the
Christian tradition nor is meditation the same as contemplative prayer. The aim of Christian meditation is
to make our minds and senses familiar with the truths
of Revelation so that this contact will move our hearts.
Meditation, like the prayer of presence, demands a mea-

sure of recollection. Yet enough "spirit-power" remains active in the senses, mind and heart to enable the person to direct them in a disciplined manner to ponder some truths of the Revelation. The Christian meditator dwells upon these truths thoughtfully. With the help of grace, she ends her meditation with an application of newly found insights to her life. This kind of meditation is also called discursive. It prevails in the beginning of the spiritual life. Yet, even in advanced stages, the Christian should return periodically to such meditation. It helps him to imbue his senses, mind and imagination with the truths of Revelation. It roots intellect, memory and will in the historical reality of Jesus' life.

To clarify further the nature of the prayer of presence, we need to distinguish theological discourse from discursive meditation. Theological discourse is the thoughtful and prayerful study of the truths of Revelation. Theologians offer us a profound understanding and a more refined expression of the truths that underpin our faith. Theological discourse conveys directives that help to guide the formation of our spiritual life.

To transform our life in Christ implies that we also transform our secular knowledge and experience. Here too theology comes to our aid. Theologians try to connect contemporary knowledge and experience with Christian Revelation. One fruit of this dialogue may be a more lucid understanding of Revelation itself and a new formulation of its hidden richness. However, intellectual understanding alone would not be sufficient for spiritual formation in depth. Unless this insight is assimilated into our heart, it may remain only head-knowledge. As such, it cannot foster formation in Christ nor can it be adapted to the unique apostolic situation we find ourselves in.

This assimilation of theological insight is fostered by fidelity to spiritual exercises such as discursive meditation. The aim of theology is not to nourish directly our spiritual life. Theology nourishes first of all our faith-enlightened intellect whereas meditation on a scriptural, liturgical, spiritual or theological text may touch more directly our heart.

In this meditation we shift from a primarily intellectual approach to one that is intuitive-spiritual. Scriptures, liturgical texts, and certain writings of the spiritual masters are filled with images, life stories, and the wisdom of everyday living in faith. The life knowledge they convey surpasses conceptual knowledge in that it can inspire and move the reader to concrete acts of faith, hope and love.

Living wisdom, imagery and symbolism appeal to the whole of human and spiritual life. Theological concepts, if not understood, require further study. Their primary purpose is to deepen rational understanding of Revelation, which in turn may prepare for more profound faith-understanding. Images, symbols or sacred words are not conceptual in the same sense. Only part of their truth is revealed to the person meditating on them. They tend, however, to sink deeply into the consciousness of the person. Slowly but surely, by meditative repetition, they communicate inner faith meanings that can transform one's life. Faith forms the whole person if this gift is taken up in graced appropriation. These images and symbols radiate their influence through prayerful reminiscence and formative repetition. Let us take as an example a meditation on the birth of Jesus.

The mystery of Jesus' birth in Bethlehem invites meditative dwelling. In this case it is not a fact to be demonstrated or a problem to be reasoned out.

The truth that interests us at this moment is not primarily intellectual. In discursive meditation, we consider prayerfully and repeatedly various facets of the mystery of incarnation. This faithful consideration nourishes our loving presence to the Lord. Graced by God in such meditative dwelling, our will may be moved to acts of love and surrender, thanksgiving and praise.

In theological discourse the student asks himself how one can understand the mystery of incarnation intellectually. How were the divine and the human united in one person? Was the God-man born with all our human capacities? Was he subjected to the laws of development of the human consciousness? What about his unconscious, his will, his emotionality? In theological discourse, one's attitude is primarily that of grasping intellectually; in discursive meditation it is one of becoming ready to be grasped.

Discursive Meditation and the Prayer of Presence

Discursive meditation may move into brief or prolonged moments of prayerful presence in which all inward discourse falls silent. We should not feel frightened when this happens but grateful. God is telling us at such moments that our discursive dwelling on his mysteries is now superfluous. He simply wants our hearts to be filled with silent longing for him. He is giving us what the masters have called acquired contemplation or the prayer of presence.

What we call the prayer of presence is contemplative, as distinguished from theological reflection and discursive meditation. To say this prayer is one of *acquired contemplation* means that any Christian with the help of ordinary grace can achieve this kind of presence to the Father in Jesus. What is called *infused contemplation* is a kind of presence to the Holy Trinity that can be received only as a result of a more extraordinary grace.

The prayer of presence is marked by peaceful attention. To be present is not to be empty but filled with a loving presence to the Divine, a quiet gaze on his beauty flowing into and forming our life from birth to death and beyond.

When we enter into this prayer, we suspend theological discourse. We allow the Lord to quiet for a moment our reasoning mind. We simply dispose ourselves to let the Spirit work within us in silence. As conceptualizing comes to a temporary halt, Jesus takes over as the principle agent in our soul. He takes the initiative; we wait in watchful, tranquil attention, flowing with every inspiration his Spirit may grant us. This momentary abstinence from discourse increases our receptivity for the nearness of the Lord and the touches of union he may grant us during this abiding.

Our theological knowledge of him, no matter how necessary for many other reasons, is inadequate and imperfect. In and by itself this knowledge cannot lead to the prayer of presence. St. Thomas, following Augustine, teaches that God transcends any concept or form human intelligence can conceive. In *The Ascent of Mount Carmel*, St. John of the Cross maintains: "Faith causes darkness and a void of understanding in the intellect.... For though faith brings certitude to the intellect, it does not produce clarity, but only darkness." (Book II, Chapter 6, Paragraph 2). "Everything the intellect can understand ... is most unlike and disproportionate to God...." (Book II, Chapter 8, Paragraph 5).

In the prayer of presence, we are open to God in simple faith, hope and love. He can be known by loving presence in a deeper way than he can be known intellectually. During the prayer of presence theological and discursive reasoning are only suspended, not denied, for they should be engaged in at other times and places. This suspension of analysis contributes to that inner stillness, which is even more necessary than outer silence if we are to ready ourselves for the gift of presence.

In this prayer we begin to know God more by love than by reasoning. Knowledge by love is superior to knowledge by intellect. According to St. Thomas, conceptual knowledge brings God down, so to speak, to our level. It imposes upon him the concepts we take from the surrounding world. Love, on the contrary, goes out to its object. It goes to the essence of God, to God as he is in himself. By love God may be reached in this life, but never by intellectual knowing alone.

In light of this experiential knowledge gained by love in the prayer of presence, theological knowledge of God may *seem* like ignorance. In *The Spiritual Canticle*, St. John of the Cross writes: "It seems to the soul that its former knowledge, and even the knowledge of the whole world, is pure ignorance in comparison with that knowledge" (Stanza XVII, Paragraph 11).

No person, no matter how learned, truly knows God unless he knows him by the heartfelt experience of peaceful love. The knowledge of love granted in the prayer of presence means simply that the depth of nearness engendered in the human spirit and heart by the Holy Spirit reverberates in the intellect and will. As a result, one's heart is filled with a wisdom that does not come from without, through the senses, but from within — from an abundance of silent love.

Christian spiritual life ideally implies that this graced inspiration will in turn flow out into our whole life and our environment, transforming it gently and helping to create harmony, peace and justice among people. This incarnational pole is as basic as the inspirational, though it has been neglected in certain devotional writings. Hence in the next chapter we will highlight the impact of this prayer on one's daily life in the world.

COVER ME WITH YOUR PINIONS

The one who seeks salvation
Outside you, my Lord,
Will meet with endless disappointment.
Furious pursuit of pleasure
Steals rest and gentleness,
Impatient desire
Prevents abiding peace.
Moments of fulfillment
Vanish like flowers
That delight us with their fragrance
Only to wither away.
How desperately we cling to pleasure,
How vainly we struggle
To avoid its disappearance.
And yet, Lord, we know
That all pleasure is doomed to fade,
To vanish without trace.
So fleeting is
The satisfaction of a wish
That it begins to fade
The moment we achieve
The aim we longed for anxiously.
Desires in tune with the Divine
Mellow and make gentle
This life of striving.
Engulfment by the Holy,
Silences restlessness
And frees my soul
From painful craving.
Thus, my Lord, I pray:
Cover me with your pinions,
Hide me under your wings,

Be my buckler and my shield
That I may dare to die to any selfish wish:
For the death
Of your faithful one
Is precious in your eyes.

CHAPTER 4

Practicing the Presence
of God

When we pray, we raise our hearts and minds to God
in movements of adoration, thanksgiving, petition and
pure presence. These movements signify our desire to
listen to God's will in daily life and to become attuned
to our divine life direction. They are offerings and acts
aimed at making us better instruments that God can
use in his ongoing formation of the world.

The practice of the presence of God in the midst of
everyday activity has been adhered to by many saintly
people. Their experience of this practice is recorded in
spiritual diaries, poems, essays and letters. No one is
more noted for this "contemplative work" than Brother
Lawrence of the Resurrection, a Carmelite Friar, who
lived from 1614 to 1691. As his years in religious life
progressed, Brother Lawrence lived continually in the
presence of God. He knew that we must trust God
once and for all and abandon ourselves to him alone.
In and through this abandonment, God will lead us
closer to other people and closer to the Center of ourselves. In contrast to alienation and lack of direction, we

experience a sense of communion and connectedness when God is our Center. Time is pierced by the Eternal. The Infinite invades the finite. The Transcendent gives meaning and purpose to all mundane endeavors.

Brother Lawrence practiced and taught the virtues of human helplessness, vulnerability and creatureliness. This humble stance enabled him to manifest the strength of God. His prayer life made him aware of God's mercy condescending to our misery — a basic theme of his letters, maxims, and conversations.

Despite the reality of original sin, we are created by God as good. He has made our union with him the ultimate goal of human life. Our life is to be a living prayer to the living God. This prayer, of which each human being is capable, only becomes actual if we trust in his providential goodness and accept his will or divine plan for our lives.

Brother Lawrence, who described himself as "a clumsy lummox who broke everything," was assigned menial tasks in the kitchen, but "because he broke everything," his superior transferred him to the shoe repair shop of the monastery. God gave him an affinity for this task because he suffered from chronic gout! Whereas a less humble soul might have despaired due to this lack of recognition, Brother Lawrence experienced the deepest joy. He did each task with high good spirits and thus earned a reputation for holiness that spread beyond the monastery walls. People needed to hear his message of abandonment and trust; they needed to know for sure that God never tests us beyond our ability to endure. He wrote to a priest:

> I regard myself as the most wretched of all men, stinking and covered with sores, and as one who has committed all sorts of crimes against his King. Overcome by remorse,

I confess all my wickedness to Him, ask His pardon and abandon myself entirely to Him to do with as He will. But this King, filled with goodness and mercy, far from chastising me, lovingly embraces me, makes me eat at His table, serves me with His own hands, gives me the keys of His treasures and treats me as His favorite. He talks with me and is delighted with me in a thousand and one ways; He forgives me and relieves me of my principal bad habits without talking about them; I beg Him to make me according to His heart and always the more weak and despicable I see myself to be, the more beloved I am of God. This is how I look upon myself from time to time in His holy presence. [Brother Lawrence of the Resurrection, *The Practice of the Presence of God*, trans. John J. Delaney (New York: Image Books, 1977), p. 69, See also p. 36. All references are by page number to this edition.]

Brother Lawrence states clearly the intention behind his practice of "holy presence." It is to be remade according to the heart of Jesus. This foundational theme of transformation of heart is fully developed in his letters. There we find the connection between the practice of presence and the lifting up of one's heart to the Lord.

This prayer begins when we become attentive to the "interior entreaties" grace allows to well up in our soul. In faithfulness to these Spirit-infused invitations heard deep inside, we are to respond by lifting our heart to God or by a sweet and loving gaze or by such words as love fashions on these occasions. Brother Lawrence would use "love words" like, "My God, here I am, all Yours." "Lord make me according to your heart" (p. 56). God, who is love, seems satisfied with these few words. Through them we are awakened again to his presence in the depths of our soul.

The condition to receive this presence of God is that of emptiness: " . . . the heart must be emptied of all other things, for God wishes to possess it alone" (p. 60). Only if we empty ourselves inwardly of all that is not God can he act there and do as he wishes. Though our minds and feelings may resist, we are to withdraw into the deep recesses of our heart. Distraction, agitation, fear, nervous tension — all must give way to the flow of quiet presence. Especially in the midst of our troubles, we are to take solace in God as often as we can. Brother Lawrence assures us:

> Lift up your heart to Him during your meals and in company; the least little remembrance will always be most pleasing to Him. One need not cry out very loudly; He is nearer to us than we think (p. 65).

This art of the "least little remembrance" encourages us to be present to God. No complicated methods are needed. Nor is it always necessary to be in Church, for "we can make a private chapel of our heart where we can retire from time to time to commune with Him, peacefully, humbly, lovingly . . . " (p. 65). We can begin at any moment, for God is there, awaiting a "single generous resolution from us."

Adoration of God in the prayer of presence demands that we offer him our heart from time to time (during the day at special interludes or in the midst of our work). What suffices is a little remembrance of him, some interior gaze or word. The mind at this point is in the heart, rather than the heart being in the mind. Once the heart is transformed by the power of prayer, our thoughts shall frequently turn to God, for where our heart is there too our treasure lies.

The peace we feel in his presence encourages us to engage from time to time in intimate, loving, humble conversation with him. To prevent our minds from wandering away, we "must make our hearts a sanctuary where we adore Him continually, (p. 94). This earnest devotion facilitates emptying our minds and hearts of all else so that in these moments of presence God alone can be the center of our attention. Then our heart becomes like the heart of Jesus, who suffered obediently that the Father might raise him to glory.

Union with the suffering heart of Jesus is another theme in the spirituality of Brother Lawrence. He experienced and believed in the redemptive power of suffering whether physical or spiritual. In his letters he refers not only to many bodily ailments but also to long periods of aridity. During the first ten years of his religious life, he endured a lengthy desert experience. He lived in continual dryness and felt only the absence of God. Suddenly one day his good will was rewarded. God granted him a profound experience of peace and joy — a presence to the Divine Presence that transformed his pain into an ineffable happiness that stayed with him for the rest of his life. Nothing could shake his confidence in God or change the fact that he had found his Center (p. 68).

> I do not know what God wishes to do with me, I am always very happy; everybody suffers and I who deserve the most severe punishments, I feel joys so continual and so great that I am scarcely able to contain them (p. 90).

This peace in the midst of pain characterized the rest of his life and became the special mark of his genial, gentle holiness. He discovered that the best way to cope with suffering was not via stoic indifference or pessimistic complaint but constant conversation with God in all matters, great or small, at all times and in all places.

One may pause anytime during the day to bring God to the forefront of our thoughts — to praise his name, to tell him of our love, to reaffirm our desire to do his will, to ask him for what we need. Such prayers may be few and short, but they are manifestations of the aura of deep presence in which we live.

The prayer of presence thus implies an ever deepening orientation of one's entire life to God. This simple interior gaze of love satisfies our longing for union in ways beyond our imagining. This gaze signifies that we see God and his glory in everything; that we accept ourselves as his beloved creatures and suffer all kinds of miseries for love of him; that we depend wholly on grace and the help of God for the fulfillment we seek; that without him we are and can do nothing.

The art of practicing the presence of God means at every moment to live the Paschal Mystery, to be present to the Passion, Death, and Resurrection of our Lord. This practice is, therefore, a foundational element of Christian spirituality. The prayer of the heart is not an elite enterprise for a chosen few but a way of life within reach of all. It is not a pious exercise but a way of living faith modeled on Christ.

This prayer presupposes two attitudes: watching and waiting. The person who lives in awareness of the Divine Presence guards or watches over his heart, that is, he centers his feeling, functioning, aspiring life in the Father and his will. This person waits upon the slightest directive God communicates through the situations of daily life. She waits even in the darkness, trusting that God is near and will reveal himself in good time. He waits for God to lead him through the agony of aridity to the joy of experienced communion with the Risen Lord. He waits for his grace to sustain him when he feels lonely and forsaken. She waits upon the Holy Spirit who prays in her when human words cease.

The prayer of the heart does not stay closed in upon

itself. It flows over into heartfelt love for others and into loving dedication to our daily task. Like Brother Lawrence, we are glad to do any task, however menial, for the love of God. No matter what we are doing on the surface, we are absorbed in God in the core of our being. In the everyday, ordinary, mundane activities that take up our time, we see a potential for the turn to transcendence — that is, we see work not as an end in itself but as a channel through which we incarnate our obedience to God's will. We see that small things of life done lovingly for God grant us a spirit of inner liberation. This freed spirit in turn clarifies our reasons for doing what we do. The root of our motivation is God and his image and form in our soul. His Spirit frees our spirit from undue worry, for we try not to lose sight of God. The faithfulness he shows to us enables us to overcome the fear of failure, for no matter how many faults we have, we are assured of God's forgiveness.

These foundational elements are summarized in the *Fourth Conversation*, dated November 25, 1667 (pp. 48-51). In this conversation, Brother Lawrence describes his way of going to God. It consists of several steps that begin with an act of radical detachment or the once and for all renunciation of everything that we know does not lend itself to facilitating our journey to God. This renunciation may seem negative, but it really implies a positive recommitment to our Christian formation tradition and the values it insists will transform our heart.

This renunciation/recommitment will be easy if we accustom ourselves to continual conversation with Christ, a conversation of utmost simplicity, free of intricate reasoning. Knowing by faith that God is intimately present in us, we can address ourselves to him at every moment. In this conversation, we ask his aid, discern his will in doubtful things, and promise to do well those things we see clearly that he is asking. We offer what we do to God before doing it and we give him thanks for having done it. Unceasingly, we praise, adore and love God for his goodness and perfection.

We are to rely on the power of Christ with complete confidence. That is, we are to ask for his grace regardless of our sins, knowing that he never fails to grant us the help we need. Brother Lawrence believes that our growth in holiness will partly depend on doing for God what we ordinarily do to draw attention to ourselves. The best way of reaching God is doing ordinary tasks in this spirit. Whatever our state of life obliges us to do — cleaning cutlery, repairing shoes, writing letters of spiritual counsel — all of these unassuming duties, from the most difficult to the most mundane, Brother Lawrence said *do lightheartedly*. He insisted that we should not divide our life into prayer time and work time but that we are called to union with God *always*.

Our prayer may consist simply of this awareness of the presence of God in the core of our being. There we are oblivious to everything but love. Strangely enough, this inner closeness energizes us to meet outer commitments with zest and joy. We are less inclined to get into a slothful slump. The deadness that pervades so many people's lives is replaced by the joy of new birth in Christ. These same people marvel at our energy, wondering from what source it comes. Brother Lawrence knew, as we know also, that the secret is Christ.

We must never weary, he says, of doing little things for the love of God, for he looks not at the grandeur of our actions but at the love with which they are performed. This love strengthens us to endure the sufferings he may send, for we have surrendered our will to him, convinced that he will never fail us. It may be difficult in the beginning to acquire this stance of total surrender, but as we grow in presence to God, so too grows our love. Brother Lawrence discovered that performing our duties for him becomes an effortless task that gives us great pleasure. All else is but a bridge to be passed over quickly in order to lose ourselves by love in him who is our final destination.

Union with the will of the Father — this is the basis of Christian living. The end of our lives is to become the most perfect adorers of God we can be. It is to grow with Christ in charity, hope, faith. It is to recognize in the end that perfection depends on his grace — for he is the sculptor who has formed us from the beginning to live in his image and likeness. As Brother Lawrence recalls:

> Sometimes I think of myself as a block of stone before a sculptor, ready to be sculpted into a statute, presenting myself thus to God and I beg Him to form His perfect image in my soul and make me entirely like Himself.
>
> At other times, as soon as I concentrate, and with no trouble or effort on my part, I feel my whole spirit and my whole soul raised up and it remains so as if suspended and firmly fixed in God as its center and place of rest (p. 70).

From the life and teachings of Brother Lawrence, we have seen that prayer is a way of being, a mode of presence to the Divine Presence, that finds expression in different ways. At times it is a cry of anguish and torment, arising from the abyss of human loneliness and desolation.

> As the hind longs for the running waters,
> so my soul longs for you. O God.
> A thirst is my soul for God, the living God.
> When shall I go and behold the face of God?

My tears are my food day and night,
>as they say to me day after day, "Where is your God?"
>>PSALM 42

At other times, it is a song of joy ringing out in a moment
of unmitigated happiness.

I will extol you, O my God and King,
>and I will bless your name forever and ever.
>>PSALM 145

Zion is my resting place forever,
>in her will I dwell, for I prefer her.
I will bless her with abundant provision,
>her poor I will fill with bread.
Her priests I will clothe with salvation,
>and her faithful ones shall shout merrily for joy.
>>PSALM 132

And, of course, prayer can become a wordless peace
that invades our inmost being because we are at one
with God. As Brother Lawrence wrote, " . . . I know only
that God protects me, I am in a state of tranquillity so
sublime that I fear nothing. What could I fear when I
am with Him? I hold fast to Him as much as I can; may
He be blessed by all, Amen" (p. 73).

Prayer is many ways, yet it is one. It is always the
soaring of the spirit of man to meet and be with the
Spirit of God. It is human heart calling to Sacred Heart.
It is the alone with the Alone. Only if God fills our hearts
can we fill the world with him. As Brother Lawrence has
taught us, the condition for being made full is that we
become empty — empty of egoism and as powerless
as the Crucified Christ. For it is in the misery of our
powerlessness that we call down upon ourselves and
others the Infinite Glory and Mercy of God.

As long as we remain our own measure, as long as
we take pride in our power and flex the muscles of our

projects, we remain far away from God. Only when we allow his Paschal Mystery to live in us, only when we take up our cross and follow him, can we abide always in his Presence. Only then can we allow God to be God in our lives, confounding human wisdom by divine foolishness, turning our nothingness into living fire. This is what God did to Brother Lawrence, to St. Therese of Lisieux and to a host of other saints. It is what he will do to us, if we become not merely people who pray but living prayer.

This state of transformation is not a luxury reserved for a holy elite. It is the condition all Christians are called to. As the body needs breath, so the spirit needs prayer. Through and in prayer, we are related to God, to Christ, to ourselves, to one another, to the here and now, and to all that is to come. This relation is dynamic, constantly growing, deepening, changing. We do not know exactly how our lives are going to turn out; we know only that we must keep on following his call. And so with Moses, we ask, "Who art Thou?" With Mary, "How shall this be done?" With the disciples, "Where do you live? What would you have me do?"

God's answers, communicated to his little ones, are personal and mysterious. Truth is made clear, though mystery remains. Light dawns through pervading darkness. Joy erupts amidst pain. We discover that this ongoing interplay of presence, absence and deeper presence is God's way of loving. Who could refuse his call?

THE SPLENDOR OF YOUR PRESENCE

Lord,
You want me to learn from you
Gentleness of heart.
No matter how I fail you,
Your gentleness never fails me.
You are slow to anger;
Your kindness is without limit.
You tell me not to be distressed,
To make your gentleness my own
So that my soul may find rest.
Give me the wisdom to make time in my day
For a gentle nursing of my soul.
Free me from arrogance,
From goals too sublime for me.
Still and quiet my soul
As a mother quiets the little ones on her lap.
Free me from the need for achievement.
Make my life less forceful, more gentle,
Centered in you alone.
Let the splendor of your presence
Light up my everydayness.
Make me a smooth channel for the outflow
Of your Divine Will in this world.
Let me move gently
In the omnipresence of the Divine.
Harmonize my frail spirit with the Infinite Spirit
Who fills the universe and its history.
Love of my Lord,
Invade my soul and melt away any trace of vehemence.

CHAPTER 5

Silence and Presence

When peaceful silence lay over all,
and night had run the half of her swift course,
down from the heavens, from the royal throne,
  leapt your all-powerful Word;
into the heart of a doomed land the stern warrior
  leapt.

(Ws. 18:14–15)

This familiar quote from the Book of Wisdom reveals the relation between silence and presence in the life of the Christian. Silence connotes a state of readiness, a time of waiting, a direction of attention. In silence we ready ourselves to receive the word God utters in the "depths of our heart. We await in silent anticipation his hoped for appearance. All of our attention is attuned to the presence. At moments like this life itself unfolds in hushed silence. We listen for the Word spoken by the Father as intensely as dry soil longs for rain. In this silence we welcome the least manifestation of God's presence.

Silence is not an empty state but a world of meaning in itself. Out of the deep interior silence characteristic of the prayer of presence words arise that are full of meaning: poetic and prophetic words. Silence invites true saying or reflective speech as distinct from mere talkativeness. Silence is the space out of which flows contemplation and action, wonder and word.

If we doubt the power of silence as a world in itself, we can turn to the philosopher Max Picard, who affirms that "silence is not simply what happens when we stop talking." It is not a condition we can produce at will because "silence is an autonomous phenomenon." He writes:

> It is therefore not identical with the suspension of language. It is not merely the negative condition that sets in when the positive is removed; it is rather an independent whole, subsisting in and through itself. It is creative, as language is creative; and it is formative of human beings as language is formative, but not in the same degree.
>
> Silence belongs to the basic structure of man. [Max Picard, *The World of Silence* (South Bend, Ind.: Gateway Editions, 1952), p. 15. All references are by page number to this edition.]

To restore our appreciation of language, Picard says, it is necessary to uncover the world of silence, for when the word loses its connection with its silent source, language becomes emaciated. The word thus emerges from the silence, and only in silence can we hear the word.

> Speech came out of silence, out of the fullness of silence. The fullness of silence would have exploded if it had not been able to flow out into speech.
>
> The speech that comes out of silence is as it were justified by the silence that precedes it. It is the spirit that legitimizes speech, but the silence that precedes speech is the pregnant mother who is delivered of speech by the creativity activity of the spirit. The sign of this creative activity of the spirit is the silence that precedes speech.
>
> Whenever a man begins to speak, the word comes from silence at each new beginning (p. 24).

To be a true speaker and doer, a person, according to Picard, must be present to the creative activity of the spirit in silence. Again we discover that the practice of presence is the best preparation for action and participation. Speaking at length offers not the slightest guarantee that understanding will be advanced, that good works will be done. If anything, idle speculation, chatter and gossip are likely to take over. Only if we can dwell in silent presence do we have a chance to say and do something of value.

The most profound silence is that deep interior state of presence that Thomas Merton calls the "mother of Truth." To prepare for this silence, it is good to cultivate the art of attention, that is, not merely the physical absence of noise or chatter but an attentive inner stilling that holds us in a state of readiness. When our minds are free of mental clutter, we are more ready to make room for God. His presence is likely to be crowded out by the discord of confused thoughts, idle expectations, or compulsive urges by which we reduce mystery to our finite concepts. Ideally, attentive silence or inner stilling ought to open our inner ears so that we can hear the voice of God in deep interior silence. This is the silence in which the mysteries of God are revealed to us, for ...

> it is in silence that the first meeting between man and the Mystery of God is accomplished, and from silence the word also receives the power to become extraordinary as the Mystery of God is extraordinary (p. 228).

This mystery that is the "mother of Truth" surrounds Jesus as he stands in defenseless attention before the Sanhedrin.

> Eventually two stepped forward and made a statement, "This man said, 'I have power to destroy the Temple of

God and in three days build it up.' " The high priest then stood up and said to him, 'Have you no answer to them? What is this evidence these men are bringing against you?' But Jesus was silent. (Mt. 26:60-63).

Was Jesus' silence not indicative of his profound contemplative presence to the Father? Jesus was not listening to the surface noise around him but to the voice of the Father. He was wholly absorbed in his will and not in need of defending this Mystery before the ranting mobs. His silence became an active witness to the Eternal.

Merton's reflections from *Thoughts in Solitude* (New York: Image Books, 1968, p. 84) help us to understand why Jesus remained silent.

> When we have lived long enough alone with the reality around us, our veneration will learn how to bring forth a few good words about it from the silence which is the mother of Truth.

> Words stand between silence and silence; between the silence of things and the silence of our own being. Between the silence of the world and the silence of God. When we have really met and known the world in silence, words do not separate us from the world nor from other men, nor from God, nor from ourselves because we no longer trust entirely in language to contain reality.

> Truth rises from the silence of being to the quiet tremendous presence of the Word. Then, sinking again into silence, the truth of words bean us down into the silence of God.

> Or rather God rises up out of the sea like a treasure in the waves, and when language recedes His brightness remains on the shores of our own being.

Jesus lived for thirty years alone with the reality around him. His veneration for the goodness of the Father, expressed in the goodness of Mary and Joseph, generated the words exchanged between them. These words are not recorded in scripture, but we can be sure they came from silence, which like a pregnant mother gives birth to Truth. This Truth would be Jesus' only message during his public life. He, the Divine Word, would stand between the silence of things and the silence of our own being. There, between the silence of the world and the silence of God, stood the Incarnate Word. When the time came for him to fulfill his destiny, he would in no way try to defend his teaching, for he knew that one cannot trust entirely in language to contain reality. Words, however simple and profound, could be distorted, twisted, and used against the defendant. So he chose to remain silent. The validity of his teaching would meet the test of time. He had given it to his disciples and now he had to return to the Father. But he would not leave them orphans, for out of his quiet tremendous presence to the Father would flow the Holy Spirit, the Advocate, like a treasure in the waves. The earthly teaching of Jesus would sink into silence, but his brightness would remain on the shores of our being. The words he did speak would become our most precious gifts. Dwelling on them would lead us to the heart of his message. Then we too could enjoy the fruits of silence — presence to the Holy Trinity in a loving exchange beyond all words.

When Jesus chose to remain silent, he taught us a new kind of language, the language of pure presence where verbalizing would only prevent communication. This language goes directly from the heart of man to the Heart of God, without the mediation of words. Words come later; what suffices now is the silent gaze of love, the spirit of thanksgiving, the witness of appeal. In this depth, language is suspended temporarily. We abide silently in the presence of God, ready to receive the slightest touch of his nearness.

Such encounters beyond words can be deeply healing experiences. We are assured in them that God loves us as we are and is willing to help us become who we are meant to be.

The silence of Jesus led him to the final, most expressive action of his life: his Passion, Death and Resurrection. So, too, silence will lead us to expressive action. Such action is neither impulsive nor compulsive; it is reflective. It is action in tune with God's direction of our life and with our unique potential to realize that direction. The true follower of Jesus is not a victim of cheap sloganeering or passing opinions. He acts on the basis of wise decision made in silent consultation with the Lord.

The person whose action flows from contemplative presence is notably less agitated, less dominated by tension and stress. He appears serene, gracious, relaxed, under even the most trying circumstances. His stance connotes the silence of Jesus before the Sanhedrin. This person seems to be in tune with the silent rhythms of nature as if he is always present to the ebb and flow of the sea, to the quiet of the night where faithful ones pray to the Father in secret.

The silent person is appreciative of the passage of time and of the gift of life. She flows through her days from the silence of infancy to the silence of old age to the final silent passage from earth to heaven in death. This person radiates an aura of mystery that appeals to people. He accomplishes all his work but there is something notably different in the way he does it. He is present attentively to the here and now situation while at the same time attuned to the voice of God.

The quality of our participation in the world actually increases if we live in silence. For in silence we can assess all sides of the situation and move toward wise, long range decisions. We are less attentive to our faults and more reliant on God to be our strength in weakness. Life is no longer a struggle for power, a goal to be possessed, an isolated moment of pleasure. In silence we are present to the whole as Holy. We see everyone and everything — ourselves included — against the horizon of the Transcendent. We are open to the most profound mysteries manifested in the simple goodness of the everyday. Here we can note with Picard a relationship between silence and faith, for, as he says, "the sphere of faith and the sphere of silence belong together. Silence is the natural basis on which the supernature of faith is accomplished" (p. 227).

From this reflection we can conclude that language (the language of faith) is not meant primarily to increase the exchange of information (the knowledge of words). Faith language, welling up from silent contemplative presence, is the means by which we cross the boundary between the silence of the world and the silence of God. Its main function is to bring to the light of day a revelation given to us in the darkness of faithful presence to the Father. In silence such revelation can touch our hearts, like the sayings of Jesus in the Gospel or of the saints in their maxims and counsels.

Such language, emerging from the silence, raises and responds to the deepest questions: Why am I here? What is the meaning of my life? Where is God asking me to go? What is he asking me to do? Responses to these questions can never be exhausted by a single communication, for every answer only evokes new questions. Every answer lights up a little more the depth of meaning that is already there. Thus the life questions we ask and the answers we hope to receive are like threads bound to the spool of prayer. Of this connection Picard says:

> In prayer the word comes again of itself into silence. It is from the very outset in the sphere of silence. It is taken up by God, taken away from man; it is absorbed into silence and disappears therein. Prayer can be never-ending, but the word of prayer always disappears into silence. Prayer is a pouring of the word into silence.
>
> In prayer the word rises from silence, just as every real word rises from silence, but it comes out of it only to travel straight to God, to the "voice of the ebbing Silence" (p. 230).

Picard goes on to explain that in prayer human silence comes into relation with the higher silence of God. The word — and therefore man — is in the center between two regions of silence, the lower silence of the human and the higher silence of the divine. Outside of prayer, the silence of man is fulfilled in speech, but in prayer this silence receives its meaning and fulfillment in our meeting with the silence of God. Outside of prayer, human silence serves the word, but "now, in prayer, the word serves the silence in man: the word leads the human silence to the silence of God" (p. 231).

We thus keep silence for the sake of speech and for the sake of God, to confess our faith and to declare His glory. [cf. Thomas Merton, *The Sign of Jonas* (New York: Image Books, 1956), p. 259]. If we love truth as our mother, then we will be lovers of silence. As St. Isaac of Nineveh says, "Silence is like the sunlight; it will illuminate you in God and will deliver you from the phantoms of ignorance. Silence will unite you to God himself."

Little wonder, then, that spiritual formation has always left room for silence. Spiritual masters agree that it is a foundational principle of the spiritual life. Without silence we cannot listen to God. We cannot pray. We cannot speak with humble conviction. Without silence speech becomes arrogant, fault finding, merely project-oriented. It is not healing but divisive. It is not pleasing to God but destructive of communal peace. If we practice the prayer of presence, we will be better able to check our speech. Is it agitated, restless, disquieted? Or is it calm, deliberate and quietly rooted in Christ, who is our Way, our Truth, our Life?

If our speaking does not meet this test, then perhaps we must listen again to the imperative of the spiritual master: Create Silence! Let it encompass everything, so that when the night in its swift course is half spent, the fierce warrior, the all-powerful Word of God, will leap into the heart of our doomed land and relieve our distress. Then we can imprint on our hearts this Maxim of Love composed by St. John of the Cross out of his profound union with God.

The Father spoke one Word, which was His Son and this Word He always speaks in eternal silence, and in silence must It be heard by the soul.

WORDS FALL SILENT

Divine Word
My springs are dried up.
Parched is the land of my life like a desert:
No trees in which birds nestle and sing
No streams in which fishes play and multiply.
Without divine waters
My life is a land that is doomed.
You, Divine Word,
In whom I am spoken from eternity.
Through whom I am created in time,
With whom I am elevated, divine;
You alone are the well
That refreshes my being.
I adore the stream of your love
Flowing into me ceaselessly.
Let the stream swell and swell
Till it sweeps
Into the farthest corners of my life.
All-powerful Word, you are a mighty flood,
A fierce warrior breaking through
The dikes of my resistance.
Divine Waters, fill me to the brim.
Let your life in me become
A refreshing stream of love
For all who approach my borders.

Eternal Word, without you
My land is wasteland.
Grant me the silence
That makes me less resistant
To your invasion.
Free me from words that are needless;
Soften my strident voice.

Teach me the gentle rhythm
Of speaking out, of keeping still.
Teach me the modest spacing,
The gentle modulation of spoken words.
Teach me the mystery
Of a silence that compasses everything.
Silence the unspoken selfish words
That dominate my life
Destroy the inner words
That keep the Word away.
Free me from the fascination
Of the words of people
Obsessed by power, pleasure, and possession.
Hide me
In that blessed night
Wherein all words
Fall silent,
All creatures
Soften to shadows.
Before that night is spent
Let me taste its consolation:
Your Presence, Divine Word,
In my life refreshed and purified.

CHAPTER 6

Obstacles to Growth in Prayerful Presence

Three practical questions that arise in relation to the prayer of presence concern the obstacles or problems of finding time to pray, of learning to pray again if this practice has been forsaken due to dryness or other reasons, and of trying to follow the biblical command to pray always.

Finding Time to Pray

Time is an ever present human reality. We ask ourselves why does it pass so quickly? How can I organize it better? What is the meaning of my birth, my life, my death? The answers to these questions elude us, for time is a mystery. The ancient wisdom tells us:

> There is an appointed time for everything,
>> and a time for every affair under the heavens.
>
> A time to be born, and a time to die;
>> a time to plant, and a time to uproot the plant.
>
> A time to kill, and a time to heal;
>> time to tear down, and a time to build.

A time to weep, and a time to laugh;
   a time to mourn, and a time to dance.

A time to scatter stones, and a time to gather them;
   a time to embrace, and a time to be far from embraces.

A time to seek, and a time to lose;
   a time to keep, and a time to cast away.

A time to rend, and a time to sew;
   a time to be silent, and a time to speak.

A time to love, and a time to hate;
   a time of war, and a time of peace.

ECCLESIASTES 3:1–8

Before delving into the problem of finding time to pray, we need to reflect in general on the mystery of being temporal selves. Man is the only creature who dates his beginning and his end. When we dwell experientially on time as presented in the biblical text and as lived concretely by us, we find, first of all, that it passes; secondly that it calls for order; and thirdly, that it can at moments be transcended. In other words, there is in human life the experience of passing time, of ordering time, and of transcending time. This latter experience happens in the prayer of presence.

Usually we experience passing time in connection with physical changes, with the process of aging. A vivid reminder of what happens occurs when we peruse the family photograph album. As the pictures fall into place year after year, we see condensed into a booklet a lifetime's labor of love. Into our mind may come the words of the poet T. S. Eliot, who wrote in *Four Quartets:*

Home is where one starts from. As we grow older
The world becomes stranger, the pattern more complicated.
Of dead and living. Not the intense moment
Isolated, with no before and after,

But a lifetime burning in every moment
And not a lifetime of one man only
But of old stones that cannot be deciphered.
There is a time for the evening under starlight,
A time for the evening under lamplight
(The evening with the photograph album).
Love is most nearly itself
When here and now cease to matter.

The photographs do not lie. Time passes, but what lasts is the love that transcends here and now, the commitment to life that burns intensely in every moment.

The experience of ordering time has a ring of daily familiarity. It is a factor rooted in the functional, managing dimension of human life. Each person reading this page knows what it is like to set the alarm clock for 7 A.M., to pencil in appointments on her pocket calendar, to decide which events have priority and to schedule them in accurate chronological order. Perhaps most of our waking time is lived according to this discipline. From its demands emerges the question, "How can I find time to pray?"

Happily for us there are also moments in human life when time is transcended. We, like the poet, experience occasions "when here and now cease to matter." Such times go beyond the chronological realm and enter the spiritual. We call them timeless moments like lovers share; like the hours spent aimlessly wandering along the shore; like the afternoons that melt into evenings under the impact of an absorbing book. At such times, without thinking about it, we are probably most intimate with God, for the eternal pierces through the temporal, the finite is immersed in the infinite.

The prayer of presence benefits from each of these time-experiences. As a prelude to it, we can utter the prayer of passing time: "Lord, don't let me fear the rapid passage of my days. Help me to see in this aging process the gentle message of your will for my life. Show me as the years go by the surest path to grace that I may see you always, in an eternal face to Face."

When schedules predominate, we can offer God, also as a prelude to presence, the prayer of immediacy: "Here I am, Lord, running from store to store to buy all the ingredients that go into tonight's meal. I have to go to the fish market, clean the vegetables, set the table — a list of orders a mile long hammers in my ear! Help me to cook a good meal and offer it to my guests as a sharing in your own creation."

And, finally, in moments of timeless transcendence, the prayer of presence may well up: "How good it is, Lord, to simply be in your presence. I love sharing with you this slowed down pace. It fills me with such peace. To see the stars, to feel the sand, to taste the breeze. Everything is caressed by you, myself included. How sweet is the mystery of life. Let me always retain something of this feeling. . . . "

In this way, there is no time in which we cannot be praying and yet, despite this experience of intimate nearness, we must be prepared for those inevitable periods of dryness that are part of the spiritual life. The temptation is to stop praying because we feel so empty; the answer is to learn to pray again.

Learning to Pray Again

To ask the question, "Can I learn to pray again?," implies that we have known the joy of praying before, though we may now be in a temporary period of aridity. What has caused this dryness to occur? On the human side it may be due to such factors as apathy, discouragement, fatigue. From the divine perspective this inability to pray may signal a new depth of relationship with God. He may be purposefully withdrawing his consolations to lead us, through absence, to experience the mystery of his presence. He may be testing our faith in this "dark night" to see if we love God as God or only for his gifts.

It is at such moments that we feel intensely our poverty of spirit. Though we could rush to fill this abyss with prayer techniques and "how to" methods, perhaps it is best to simply wait in the darkness for God's guiding light. He will lead us through this desert to a new depth of intimacy. And though we feel unable to pray, we must trust that the "Spirit scrutinizes all matters, even the deep things of God" (1 Cor. 2:10). "The Spirit too helps us in our weakness, for we do not know how to pray as we ought; but the Spirit himself makes intercession for us with groanings which cannot be expressed in speech" (Rm. 8:26).

The dying we undergo in this desert experience is meant to lead us to a new life of intimacy with God. When all else is taken away, we reach out to him in love and seek to be united to him in our prayer of silent longing. The multitude of words gives way to a peaceful telling of our love, an offering of adoration, a humble sorrow for sin. Prayer is the means by which we make room in our hearts for God. In a quiet unobtrusive way, we have to clear space inside so that our Divine Guest can enjoy an empty chamber that he may occupy to the full.

Quietly resting in God fosters not only trustful openness to the mysteries of grace within us but also relaxed in-touchness with ordinary life. The world is no longer merely the place in which we work; it is also the arena in which we worship. In patient, quiet prayer we recognize our personal need for God. We ready ourselves for his presence by humble waiting rather than babbling many words. We wait upon the Spirit who prays in us and refines our sensitivity to the Father's will.

Most of the time prayer is made in darkness. Our experience of God remains dim and obscure. We believe he is there and go on loving and adoring him though we may not feel his presence. Ours is a prayer of attentive, waiting desire — an aspiration of love reaching towards the Divine Beloved as he is in himself. It is a prayer of openness to the Lord as God, remaining steady and true in consolation as well as desolation.

Prayer is thus not to be thought of as an occasional visit to God, but as an all encompassing orientation of our being towards him in love. God remains near to us in his Spirit, though we may at times distance ourselves from him. Whether prayer is offered in petition or gratitude, in presence or absence, it is dependent on faith. In prayer God has the first initiative. He chooses the way by which each of us must go to him. To pray is to acknowledge that I am a being grasped by God and desirous of being made into a new person, into that disciple of the divine I most truly am.

A mistaken notion about the spiritual life is to think of it as made up merely of a moral code of do's and don'ts. "Athletes of asceticism" are often like the Pharisees Jesus condemns. They seek to draw attention to themselves by outward manifestations of holiness, but Jesus sees in these external shows of piety the worst possible pride. Hence he praises the prayer of the Publican, for his unassuming, humble presence reveals the childlike approach so pleasing to God.

One barrier to prayer may be the functional culture in which we live. In a world of doing, it is common to take a project-like approach to reality. The "teacher me" plans lessons. The "homemaker me" purchases the week's groceries. The "bookkeeper me" balances the monthly accounts. We may carry this same attitude of managing into prayer. We want to "do" our prayers well and even manage God. In our desire to pray again, we may be drawn to new methods and techniques of praying. We may feel that with sufficient reading, study and effort, we can attain the aim we set out to accomplish. The result inevitably is more dryness.

In true prayer of presence, the manipulative self has to recede into the background. Because prayer is a gift, it calls forth in us an attitude of expectancy and receptivity. We open ourselves to God. We allow him to touch and move us on every level of our being. We realize humbly that contemplation is not produced by a psychological technique or an intellectual process. It is a gift of grace, not attained by my efforts alone.

Prayer begins again when we unite our will to the will of the Father, whose presence we seek to embody in our day to day life situation. Prayer is saying:

Hallowed be Thy name, Father in Heaven. May Thy kingdom on earth be as real for me now as it shall be hereafter. May I do Your will in this life as I desire to do it in the life to come.

Though I may forget to ask You, sustain me in my hunger and thirst with the daily bread of life that comes to me through the grace of Your Spirit.

Though I am unworthy, I ask Your forgiveness for the times I have done things against Your will. In thankfulness to You for this forgiveness, I shall try my best to extend forgiveness to others.

Most of all, Father, guide me along the path of salvation. Deliver me from the bondage of egoism. Whenever I do get lost, grant me a little light to return to Your dwelling place with no further delay. Guided by Your light, I can sing Your praises in sorrow and joy. I can truly pray without ceasing.

Praying Always

The New Testament asks us to pray always and yet we wonder what that really means. At first sight it may seem impossible, yet we know from many examples that prayer can become a way of life, something that stays with us no matter what we are doing or thinking. How, then, can we learn to pray always?

We can only learn to pray by praying. We should not restrict ourselves to reading books about prayer, no more than lovers should be satisfied with reading books about love. We may get so wrapped up in words about how to pray that we forget to pray. Without the experience itself of prayer, words do not mean much. Moreover not everything about prayer can be put into words. Even the words of the scriptures about prayer will only mean something when we try to live and experience them.

There are many ways in which we can learn to pray always. Each way is limited. We may learn from all of them as long as we really follow the way the Spirit leads us. Some would say that to pray is to learn to talk to God. That is true, but it does not go far enough. It may give us the impression that God is a distant person. We have to learn also that he is near to us, truly within us.

Others teach prayer as conversation. That is nearer to the truth. God responds to us. The difficulty is that we cannot hear him as we can hear the voice of a friend.

It takes time to learn how to hear his silent voice in the intimacy of our heart.

To learn to pray, say others, we must learn to think about Christ, the saints, the mysteries of our faith. That makes sense too. We think about ourselves and others and what happens around us. We should think too about God and his words. That kind of prayer, or meditation, is not difficult to learn. It comes naturally to us, for we all meditate, though not always on our faith. We may meditate on the person we love, on the illness or death of a friend, on a novel we have read, on the baseball game we saw.

Meditation becomes prayerful when it focuses on the knowledge and love of God. Learning this kind of prayer helps us to gain interest in God and his word. The disadvantage of this prayer may be that we still see God as outside ourselves. We can get caught in speculations and mental games rather than learning to love and admire the Lord.

Some say that the way they learned to pray was by reflection on life. Involved as we are in our commitments, we spontaneously feel the need to muse about what happens to us during the day. We can learn to do this prayerfully by bringing God into our reflections. We sit down quietly and while the events of the day flow through our mind, we keep our heart turned to him.

Others tell us to develop a personal relationship with God. They compare that way of learning with the growth of a human relationship. It keeps growing through talking and being with another. It begins with talk and conversation; that grows into understanding one another more and more, into becoming at home with each other; finally there slowly emerges something we cannot describe in words but which reveals itself as true, lasting, love. We have simply fallen in love with God. As this love grows deeper, we need less and less words. We can be silent together and enjoy being close.

Learning to pray this way can be aided by imagining ourselves in a relation of friendship to Jesus as we know him from the Gospels. This way of prayer is excellent as long as it satisfies us. In the long run it too can have its drawbacks. God may call us gradually to a less tangible, more spiritual prayer. It would then be an obstacle in his path were we to cling to this more imaginative way of praying. It proved helpful in the beginning, but now we must let it go.

A deeper way of learning to pray is to try to live in the presence of God. This is the beginning of always praying as the Gospel and St. Paul recommend. We try in a relaxed way to become aware of his Presence all the time we are awake. We need the grace of quiet concentration and perseverance to develop this habit. Gradually awareness of his Presence becomes an underlying theme of our life, an undercurrent that never leaves us totally. This silent orientation is more spiritual and less bound to images than the former kinds of prayer. It is a matter of heeding the psalmist's directive: "Be still and know that I am God."

Learning to know God this way in prayer is not reducible to the everyday knowing of our mind. It implies making room in our heart for an experience of his loving Presence deep within us and all around us.

Learning to pray is as basic to our spiritual life as learning to breathe is for a newborn infant. Learning to pray will not always be easy. God allows periods of aridity in which praying seems empty and dull. But He also grants periods of peace and love, indescribable in their beauty.

To learn to pray, we must try in inner quiet to grow in the living faith that God is alive and at work deep within us. We must be ready to give some time and effort to prayer daily, to bear with boredom until God in his own time awakens us to his Presence.

Remaining in God's presence is the condition of always praying. There must be a way of keeping in touch with him that is open to each of us. How do we keep in touch with our family, our best friends, our beloved? We do so in many ways, via visits, postcards, letters, telephone calls, conversations, a prayer, a memory. It is necessary that we do these things enough to keep our relationship alive.

Remaining in God's presence happens in a similar way. Jesus himself gave the example. The core of his life was keeping in touch with the Father. Time and again he created moments of stillness in his life to be alone with God. These moments flowed over into the rest of his earthly existence.

He was always abiding with his Father. This presence was nourished by the words of the Hebrew scriptures he had meditated on since his youth.

To follow the way of Jesus is to create like moments of stillness in our lives. It is to pay attention to God's words as they come to us in our reading of the scriptures or in the words of the liturgy. As soon as a word strikes us as personally significant or fills us with peace, we should treasure it in our hearts. We should take it with us in our daily life and return to it again and again. It is our point of contact with the One who remains in us; it is our way of remaining in him.

We may make a collection of words and sentences

that have proven to be of help in this regard. They can serve as bridges between our busy day and the Lord within us. At any lost moment during the day, we may try to remember the words we have chosen as signposts of our presence to him. We should not reason about such words. We should allow them gently to penetrate our hearts and minds as fragrant oil saturates a sponge. Neither should we be forceful in our attention. Ours should be a stance of waiting in patience, ready to receive the imprint of the holy word in the depth of our soul, yet also ready to bear with the absence of any consolation.

What counts is a steady returning to the words of the Lord, of his Church, of his apostles and saints. This return will keep our life oriented towards him. We are truly abiding in him even if we do not feel the effects of this dwelling. In his own good time he may grant us momentary experiences of his presence. They may be fleeting but their impact is lasting. In the end we may receive the grace to pray always.

FREE AGAIN FOR YOUR PRESENCE

Grant me, Lord, the wisdom of acceptance,
Acceptance of anger I am unable to contain;
Acceptance of a life crippled and fearful
Because parents and teachers misunderstood the wis-
  dom you taught;
Acceptance of any misunderstanding instilled in me
By well meaning others.
They tried to follow your teachings
As well as they could.
But you allowed their eyes to be dimmed.
Let me remember them in compassion.
If you call me to be with children
Make me as open about my feelings
As you were with your disciples,
As Yahweh was with his chosen people.
Lord, create around me a climate of gentleness
In which each person can express himself without fear.
Let me not be tempted
To force others to pretend to feelings they do not have
Simply to please me, to make me feel good.
Teach me the art of redeemed, spiritual living.
Grant me trustworthy friends to whom I can reveal
Aggression and anger before they become too much to
  bear.
Teach me the right means to mitigate my anger
So that my soul may be free again for your presence.

Creating Conditions for Growth in Presence to the Divine Presence

Conditions for practicing the prayer of presence vary from person to person. They are many and lasting. We can begin to consider some of these from the point of view of growth in personal and spiritual maturity.

Who is the Mature Person?

While we should pray and strive for the gift of maturity, we shall never reach it completely. It is more a life orientation than a static state to be attained once and for all. We can only ask ourselves whether we are on the road to maturity. Let us dwell for a moment on the meaning of psychological maturity.

A mature person is one who has begun to care for the wholeness of her life. She tries to grow beyond the volatile impulses of childish sentiments and youthful excitements. Her life becomes less reactive and more responsive. He begins to live by wise reflection, by basic inner conviction and lasting commitment. He accepts responsibility for the life direction and life form he has discovered to be his, no matter how pedestrian or prosaic this life may seem to others. She is no longer obsessed by the extraordinary and the spectacular. Her need to be noticed, to be popular and liked, diminishes. He grows in generous solidarity with others in society and community. He accepts and copes wisely with the sufferings and limitations everyday life imposes on all human beings. She is at home with her own failures, limits, and imperfections. Without excessive guilt feelings, he tries to make the best of his life in a relaxed and gentle way. No longer does he drift off in dreams, idle fantasies, floating idealism. He forbids himself the debilitating pleasures of playing fantasy games with the harsh realities of today and tomorrow. He probes the facts and tries to improve the human situation little by little, day by day, leaving the rest in the hands of God.

What about Christian spiritual maturity? Spiritual maturity is a gift only God's grace can bestow on us. The grace of spiritual maturity usually attunes itself to our progress in psychological maturity. Our loving Creator respects the developmental phases his creatures have to go through before reaching their human maturity. He wants us to be faithful to this unfolding process of creation as it manifests itself in our lives. He lovingly allows us the time we need to grow leisurely to our spiritual ripeness in faith, in accordance with the created rhythm of our human emergence. All things in his creation unfold in their own good time. So does the human creature. A youth can live a spiritual life fully within the limits of his age and experience. He cannot yet express this life in all its possibilities unless God miraculously brings him to full maturity at an early age. Although God has done so in the case of some saints, we should not lightly expect this miracle to happen in us.

The maturity of Jesus is the measure of our spiritual maturity. St. Luke writes of him: "Jesus, for his part, progressed steadily in wisdom and age and grace before God and men" (Lk. 2:52). Notice well: Jesus grew not only to human maturity before men but also to spiritual maturity before God. Only when our Lord had reached full human and spiritual maturity, was he moved by the Spirit to begin his public life and to approach his hour with the full responsibility of a mature person who has found his unique direction.

St. Paul reminds us: "Brethren, do not be childish in your outlook. Be like children as far as evil is concerned, but in mind be mature." (1 Cor. 14:20) Can we say with Paul: "When I was a child I used to talk like a child, reason like a child. When I became a man I put childish ways aside" (1 Cor. 13:11)?

The spiritual maturity Jesus grew to and St. Paul speaks about is based upon the foundation of a full-grown faith. St. Paul describes this mature faith: "Let us, then, be children no longer, tossed here and there, carried about by every wind of doctrine that originates in human cleverness and skill...." "In this way we are all to come to unity in our faith and in our knowledge of the Son of God, until we become the perfect Man, fully mature with the fullness of Christ himself" (Ep. 4:14, 13).

A fully matured faith presupposes a personal conversion during our growing up. Such a conversion of maturity calls for a personal encounter with and an unshakable commitment to our Lord. This conversion must gradually draw our whole scattered personality into unity with the mystery of Christ's maturity.

Our conversion or wholehearted turning to Christ means that we begin to live out of a basic Christian conviction rooted in our love for him instead of living out of childish sentiment and youthful excitement, no matter how pious our "causes" may appear.

Our personal encounter with him and our subsequent commitment means that Christ becomes the lasting motivation of our life rather than any other partial or shifting motivation. Allowing our self in *all* its dimensions to be drawn into the holy maturity of Jesus means that our life becomes centered and whole, no longer carried along by the winds of incidental fads and doctrines. All of these characteristics are in accord with what we recognize as expressions of psychological and spiritual maturity. Spiritual maturity is a gift of grace, but we have to be faithful to this gift. A deep devotion to the holy maturity of Jesus can strengthen us in that fidelity.

Three problem areas are likely to present themselves as we try to remain faithful to the grace God grants us in the prayer of presence. These are anger, the experience of failure, and betrayal by others which calls for forgiveness. At first glance these problems appear to be obstacles to personal holiness. However, as we learn to cope with them in humility and faith, they reveal themselves as aids in disguise leading to the divine intimacy we seek. We will conclude this chapter with a look at the life of Francis Libermann, who exemplifies what can happen when we allow God to take our weakness and turn it into his strength.

Is Anger Always Wrong?

All people get angry, saints and sinners alike. Saints too are human. Holiness does not take away humanness. Our Lord himself shows in his anger with the Pharisees how human he was. Feeling angry is as human as feeling sad, delighted, loving, tired or lonely.

Everybody gets angry. This may not always be apparent, but it is so. The only exceptions are not saints but some people whose brain functioning is impaired. Saints get angry like everyone else. The difference is that anger does not dominate their lives. They may be incidentally angry, usually at the right time and in the right way, but they seem to know better how to handle their anger.

Growth in spiritual formation does not whittle away our capacity to feel angry. Neither does it lessen the need to respond in some way to that feeling. Spiritual formation helps us to accept our anger as a human feeling that is undeniably there.

All of us are born with the ability to feel angry. We imbibed angry reactions from others long before we could talk. We did not understand what was being said angrily by the people around us, but we could sense the angry feelings of our father and mother, brothers and sisters. We learned from them on the spot how to act angrily. As children, we also listened to the way in which they responded to our anger, when we dared to let it come out. Maybe we were among the fortunate whose families allowed them to bring their angry feelings out into the open. This aid not mean that they gave in to whatever we were angry about; it is just that they did not punish us simply for the fact that we felt that way. They accepted the reality that angry feelings

may emerge in children outside the immediate control
of their will. Anger was allowed to express itself at its
first emergence. It did not have the time to build up
inwardly into a sudden outburst or explosion.

The Holy Spirit does not destroy what emerges in
human nature as created by God. Anger is not killed
off by the Spirit but set on a new course.

We may wrongly consider that all angry feelings are
less than human. They may seem incompatible with our
spiritual formation. We may repress our awareness of
the anger that wells up inside. We are not alone in this
response. Most people have difficulty coming to terms
with their angry feelings. They fear to take those feelings in stride. Instead of working them through, they
turn them off. They do not see them as the human feelings they are. They consider them harmful as such to
the spiritual form one's life should assume.

This denial of angry feelings may not be an act of
bad will on our part. Therefore, the gift of grace can
keep growing deep within us. However, we may not
allow this grace to transform the emotional dimensions
of our spiritual life. We shut anger out of awareness as
quickly as it comes up. Therefore, we cannot lift it into
the transforming light of the Spirit. Such denial is the
opposite of formation; it only fosters deformation.

We may mask our anger with sweetness. It still
comes out as muffled annoyance. Our intention may
be honest, our desire to give gentle form to our life genuine. What is pretended is a lack of anger that is really
there.

Perhaps we fell into this trap because we pushed the
process of spiritual formation too fast. We skipped the
task of noticing our angry feelings, of bringing them to
light, of bearing with them. We did not give the Holy

Spirit room to mitigate our anger, to turn it into the right response at the right time.

Spiritual formation does not deny anger. It even helps us to bear with unreasonable anger. It enables us to advance from this affliction to the grace of humility. Humility is the foundation of spiritual transformation. Slowly we will be able to express our anger in a way that will not hurt others unnecessarily.

Anger, when denied, cannot spend its force wisely and moderately. It turns inward as a hidden explosive power. When it finally bursts out, it does so in an uncontrollable destructive way.

Spiritual formation allows anger to come out into the open and spend itself wisely. It may be relieved in a forthright talk with the Lord, with a good friend, one's husband, wife or spiritual director. Such openness drains our anger; it allows the flow of spiritual formation to continue again. After anger has been aired and dispersed in an acceptable way, formation deepens.

Spiritual formation helps us to grow into a divine view of life. We see in a new light the persons, events and things that arouse our anger. This vision of faith lessens our annoyance. It inspires its right expression.

Anger is likely to emerge in discomfort, disappointment, pain or frustration. We see this in the angrily crying infant who feels wet, hungry or bothered by a safety pin that has become unclasped. He expresses his discomfort wildly. He *is* his anger, as it were. He cannot as yet develop a wider view of life. He is unable to mitigate his anger or to disperse it completely, whereas an adult who has gone through the channels of formation can do just that.

It is not enough to cultivate this wider vision. We must also know the source of our anger. Only then can we see it against the horizon of faith and let it be tempered accordingly.

First of all, we must admit freely that we feel angry. Next we need to find out why we feel this way. Only then can we do something about it. Our angry "feeling against" can be tempered by a deeper "feeling for." My feeling threatened by certain people can lessen in light of the faith experience of my being cared for by an Eternal Lover.

Gentleness creates the right climate for formative living. Moments of anger should only be interruptions in our basic style of gentle Christ-like formation. Our practice of the prayer of presence may deepen to such a degree that moments of anger no longer touch our inmost being. There Jesus' peace prevails.

We cannot force this grace. We can only wait for it in humility. Perhaps we will not be allowed to master our anger during this lifetime. In no way does this mean that we will be less graced in the depths of our being. No matter how poorly we succeed in mastering upsurges of anger, grace keeps growing in us. What counts for God is our attempt to form ourselves in the image of his Son.

God loves the humility with which we accept our failure. Acceptance is not resignation. It is cooperation with the mysterious rhythm of God's formation of our uniqueness. It is submission to God's own good time here or in the hereafter. At times he may grant us the grace to grow beyond unmitigated anger. To refuse that grace would be a sign of bad faith, to push beyond it a sign of arrogance. We must accept the limits of progress an Infinite Love allows in our life. The pace of our transformation is set by his wisdom. To get angry about our anger only compounds the problem. It also displays lack of submission to the pace of change the Lord allows in each person's life.

When We Fail Humanly, Do We Grow Spiritually?

Failure is an experience that affects all levels of life. A woman once served as head of a fund-raising committee for a charitable organization. She was asked to plan a campaign that had to be presented for approval to the Board of Directors. Intense work for several weeks yielded what she thought was the ideal way to go. The great day arrived to defend her proposal and much to her dismay the Board flatly rejected it. Later, as she sorted out her feelings, she learned a lot about failure.

Fatigue and failure go hand in hand. She felt drained of energy. She doubted momentarily her ability to function well in this position. Anger, irritability, resentment — these negative emotions surfaced heatedly. She experienced an effect on her spiritual life as well. It was difficult that day to become recollected and to pray without distraction. She could have easily slipped into a vicious circle of introspection, had it not been for a previous history of meditative reflection. Why did failure, which is perfectly human, lead to these bad feelings? Perhaps it is because we value success so highly.

How can we cope with failure and success from a spiritual perspective? This question alerts us to the paradoxical realization that success, from the viewpoint of transcendence, can be a failure experience! In other words, failure on the human level may feel like a curse but on the level of spiritual unfolding it can be a blessing in disguise.

For instance, bodily success, in the form of good health, abounding energy, physical beauty, inclines us to forget our finite limits. We seek the gratification of looking good, being liked, making an impression. We may use our charms to win friends and influence people. We may go so far as to make pleasure our god. Then life deals us a crushing blow. We get sick, gray hair appears; the aging process sets in. Such vital failure happens whether we will it to or not. It is a good reminder that we are finite and vulnerable. In that sense failure can facilitate spiritual unfolding.

A similar turn takes place on the functional level. There success is measured by achievement, status, financial remuneration. Competition replaces compassion. Society insists that we must be on the winning side. We mock the losers of the world. We venerate the workaholics. As long as we are climbing the ladder to success, we feel worthwhile.

Before long the resistances of life intervene. Projects we counted on never come to conclusion. Business partners betray one another. The specter of failure casts a shadow over our best laid plans. Such functional failure can also lead to meditative reflection. We begin to reset our priorities, seeing ourselves less as a product and more as a person valued in God's eyes, not just for what we do but for who we are.

This shift to the spiritual perspective shows us the relative value of success or failure in God's eyes. The Pharisee, who was the symbol of human success, was a failure before God in comparison to the humble Publican.

We need to overcome our fear of failure by transforming our response from one that is destructive to one that is constructive. This means that instead of viewing failure as a source of discouragement, we see it as a stimulant for hope. Models for this positive move are all the members of Alcoholics Anonymous, who pray: "God give me the serenity to accept the things I cannot change, the courage to change the things I can, and the wisdom to know the difference."

Instead of making failure an occasion for self-flagellation, we can see it in faith as a condition for spiritual progress, for setting more realistic goals within our God-given limits. It is the refusal of these limits that often leads to failure and the flight into fantasy. Real success involves being realistic about the concrete limitations within which human freedom must develop.

Destructive responses to failure include becoming defensive, blaming others, growing bitter. Constructive responses, by contrast, celebrate human facticity and limits as concrete proofs of the need for redemption.

Failure is not an enemy but a friend since it binds us together as a community of sinners in need of salvation. In fact failure can be a graced avenue to faith — that faith which tells us this world is not the final home of freedom. It can lead to hope — that promise that in the end we shall enjoy a new life purified by God of all earthly limits. Most of all accepting failure means growing in love — love for the limited self I am and the Limitless God in whom I live.

This constructive response to human failure is depicted in a text entitled, *Light Upon the Scaffold: The Prison Letters of Jacques Fesch.* The author recounts for us his crime, imprisonment, and pending execution. The months he spent in prison awaiting the outcome of his trial were months of intense spiritual growth. By all human standards he was an abject failure, but under the impetus of grace his spirit climbed to levels of union most of us may never experience. On the eve

of his death, he wrote to his spiritual director a letter
that reveals how at peace he was with himself and with
the world that classified him a despicable criminal:

> When you read this letter, I shall already be in heaven
> looking on Jesus. Before that happens, the grain of wheat
> must be ground by the millstones and the grape must be
> pressed, but what is there for me to fear when I have Jesus?
> I await in the night and in peace for the powers of dark-
> ness to hurl themselves upon me and slay me.... As a light
> breath of wind uproots a spring flower, so the divine gar-
> dener will come and pluck my soul to take it to paradise. Be
> sure, brother, *only a few more hours of struggle and I shall know*
> *what love really is!* Jesus suffered so very greatly for me, and
> now in his goodness he has relieved me of so much of my
> suffering that I have very little left to endure. Dear brother,
> I wait expectantly for love; I wait to become intoxicated by
> torrents of delight and to sing eternal praises to the glory
> of the risen Lord...God is Love! [Ed. Augustin-Michel
> Lemonnier (Indiana: Abbey Press, 1975), pp. 144-145.]

If ever a man could have harbored resentment
against his captors, it was Jacques Fesch, yet he chose to
forgive them. His example stands before us as we ask
a final formative question.

How Can We Forgive Someone
Who Has Wronged Us Deeply?

How many times has this question been asked by the
child whose father or mother beat her? By the wife
whose husband betrayed her? By the friend whose
solemn confidence was broken? In such cases we feel
diminished to the very core of our being. We feel de-
humanized, unloved, and justifiably angry. Our first
reaction is to seek revenge — either openly if we are
strong enough to fight back, or in silent resentment if

we are too weak. Indeed on the mere human level it seems impossible to forgive such scarring injuries.

It is for this reason that we must rise beyond the human level and turn our hearts toward the Spirit of Jesus. When someone hurts us badly, we have to break the impulse to get even by the remembrance of Jesus. Was anyone ever more wronged than he? His own disciple turned him over to the authorities, adding insult to injury by betraying him with a kiss. In face of the fickle crowds who were his friends one day and his foes the next, he would teach such lessons as: turn the other cheek; make peace with your brother before you approach the altar; forgive your enemy not seven times but seventy-seven. On the cross, when he could have vilified the soldiers and ranted angrily at the mob, he whispered quietly, "Father, forgive them; they do not know what they are doing" (Lk. 23:34).

Despite the New Testament injunction to forgive others from our heart, we often live by the primitive "eye for an eye, tooth for a tooth" mentality. This attitude seldom expresses itself in physical outbursts that in the end might be more honest. Often a hidden resentment begins to poison our life. We fail to recognize that the person who hurts us is himself in need of healing. So in mock charity we tell him, "I'll forget about what you did but don't expect me to forgive you." The trouble is that forgetting about an incident that causes such tension is not enough. We have to move toward forgiveness. Our hardened hearts resist this magnanimous movement, and so again we must turn to our Lord.

His prayer on the Cross teaches us that forgiveness has to be an act of our whole person. It cannot be merely a mental or an emotional gesture. When the young adult slowly discovers the deformative influence of a parent or teacher on his life, when he finds that for his entire life he has been on a guilt trip, he is bound to feel bitter. Discovering the cause of his anxiety is only one step in the healing process. Its completion only occurs when he is able to forgive him or her not in his mind only, but with his whole heart. An even bigger step is to see in faith that this person was placed in his life by providence for a reason and that despite the injury he received, all things work together in God for the good.

With the Lord's help, we may try to express our forgiveness in some way. Such expression can be painful or embarrassing but at least it is worth the effort. If the other refuses to accept this work of reconciliation, so be it. We know before God that the bitterness is gone from our heart, and we can pray that someday the other party may experience the same peace.

Involved in forgiveness, besides attempted expression and inner reconciliation, is a gradual letting go of any lingering displeasure we may feel towards the other for what he has done to us. The difficulty lies in the impulse we feel to preserve *my* reputation, *my* property, *my* ideas. The need for ego-preservation is powerful; that is why it can prevent us from truly forgiving the other, that is, not only saying, "I forgive you," but letting go of the displeasure we feel.

One obstacle to guard against is our tendency to make the other the *object* of *my* forgiveness. I do not really regard him as a person, but simply as a bad object whom I, in my great generosity, can forgive.

By the same token, we can refuse forgiveness or prevent it from happening within us if we reduce a person to her actions only — as if the whole of her can be summed up by what she did or did not do. If that happens, it might be impossible for us to forgive the other. We see only his weakness and overlook entirely his virtues and good will. Maybe he thought he was doing us a favor and instead we felt incensed. We bypass his intentions and merely identify him with the wrong we feel he did to us.

We can also fail in true forgiveness when we falsely forgive the other for the sake of preserving and promoting our ideal self-image as "the always-forgiving one." Such condescension is not forgiveness. It can really frustrate the other person, making her feel guilty and uncomfortably beholding to us.

Forgiveness can also be used as a means to manipulate the other by making him feel guilty. The proverbial example would be the chronically ill mother, whose son or daughter nurses her. On the one night he or she decides to go out, the mother moans, "Have fun, but if I should have one of my attacks, don't worry. I forgive you."

In the end, genuine forgiveness emerges from the conviction that I and the other are already "foregiven." Jesus is always forgiving us. We have a relatively small part to play after all. The other has already been forgiven by Christ in his act of ransoming us from sin. If we can remember that, then it may not require such a great effort on our part to forgive. Our forgiveness of the other is only a participation in what Jesus has already done.

A man who abandoned his weakness wholly into the hands of the Lord was Francis Libermann, a spiritual master of the first half of the nineteenth century. His main message is the key to growth in personal holiness: abandonment to the Father so that we may overcome our abandonment of soul.

The Spiritual Joy of Abandonment

To appreciate the message of Ven. Libermann, we should be aware of the many failures he himself experienced. He was born on April 12, 1802, the son of Lazarus Libermann, a noted rabbi. As a boy he shared the social abandonment Jewish families felt at that time. Growing up, he also faced the spiritual abandonment of a crisis of faith. Though a rabbinical student, he began to doubt the Bible. This trial ended with an apparent failure since he betrayed his heritage and converted to the Catholic faith.

Francis felt called to the priesthood and was accepted as a student in the seminary of St. Sulpice in Paris. There he underwent another trial caused by a cruel ailment, then called the "falling sickness." He began to suffer epileptic convulsions. A victim of this sickness could not be advanced to orders. So he was kept as an assistant to the bursar of the seminary and asked to do inconsequential chores around the house. Running errands in Paris, he recalls never having crossed the bridges over the Seine without the urge to cast himself into the waters below. Even within his room he dared not keep a knife or other sharp object. The only thing that saved him from despair was abandonment to God.

After ten years of suffering, he was sufficiently cured to be ordained a priest. In the meantime he had founded a religious community. Initially, it would care for abandoned souls in some of the colonies of France. Later on, he dissolved this community and allowed it to be absorbed in the already existing educational community of the Spiritans. In this way he extended his care for the abandoned to students, teachers and scholars. In the end he propagated an unbelievable variety of other works for abandoned souls in his home country. Gradually, he discovered the range of his call to the universal Church. It was disclosed to him in and through his trying out ever new works that he should aid all kinds of "abandoned souls."

Many of his followers could not immediately grasp the steady deepening of his life direction. Instead they would fixate on some initial work accepted by him that embodies only one facet of his vision. Until the end of his life, he suffered off and on some form of betrayal by his followers. He foresaw that this betrayal would even repeat itself after his death.

Libermann's spirituality originates in his experience that a person achieves his unique life form only when he abandons himself to his divine life direction. This abandonment implies an acceptance of one's nature with all its gifts and limitations. This acceptance means, for Francis, also care for our bodily welfare. He developed a whimsical formula of the three H's: health, head, and holiness. The order is significant. Grace enables and sustains this unfolding of what is best in our nature: "God gives grace, diversifying it according to the character, the mind, the natural temperament of each person. Hence everyone has his own pathway, his own direction to follow in going to God...." Francis frowned on a multitude of petty devotions or involvement in numerous ascetical practices. Without engaging in a pragmatic training in the separate virtues, he recommends remaining in the presence of God in whom all that is best in every person lies hidden in its sacred source. The rest follows spontaneously. We have called this the prayer of presence.

We are all too often at the mercy of momentary

impressions. Francis insists on calm and equanimity. Serenity facilitates abandonment to our divine life direction. It fosters abandonment as well to the unique direction of others. "When we allow everyone to act according to his own concepts, his own character, his own cast of mind, and his entire make-up, a great deal of good will be achieved." The same abandonment to God's direction made him suspicious of perfectionism.

> Beware of that imagination which makes you demand perfection in human beings, in organizations, and in things in general . . . we will encounter imperfection wherever we encounter human beings . . . let's not break anything in the process. Otherwise, we lose twenty times more than we gain in the end . . . I have observed that the really great saints always acted in the way I have recommended. Only the "petty saints," the ones who haven't gone very far along the road of piety, act contrariwise. . . . This sort of energy has another defect. It has a penchant for methods and remedies that are radical. Now, radicalism is good and even necessary in the realm of dogma, but it is detestable and destructive of all good when it comes to the administration and supervision of sacred things.
>
> Be particularly careful to overcome the embarrassment you may feel . . . in the company of men of the world. . . . Such embarrassment engenders a sort of stiffness, a kind of shyness that gives one the air of being ill-humored and stand-offish . . . you ought to like all people, no matter how they may feel about religious principles or about you . . . there is no one in this world who can even slightly force the consciences, wills, or minds of his fellow men. God didn't want to do it, why should we? (p. 267)*

For Francis the main condition and the finest fruit of this spirituality of abandonment was an attitude which he described over and over again. He called it

---

*For a complete rendition of the life of Francis Libermann, see Adrian van Kaam, *A Light to the Gentiles* (Denville, N.J.: Dimension Books, Revised Edition, 1978). All quotes are from this edition.

"douceur," a term which could perhaps be translated as gentleness. This gentleness, resulting from abandonment, creates inner harmony and peace; it excludes harshness, tension, compulsion, and rigidity towards oneself and others. It moderates all agitation, relieves anxiety, controls aggressiveness and hostility. It is the fruit of that graced self-possession gained through daily growth in the prayer of presence and abandonment to the Holy One who wills our good and lovingly guides us along the way of our divine life direction.

MIRROR OF YOUR LOVE

Lord,
The earth lights up
As a symbol
Of your presence;
All nature is suffused
With your light and life.
Let everything of beauty
Evoke in me
Loving gentility:
Each one is a reflection
Of your eternal splendor,
Each one a mirror
Easily dimmed
If I don't tend it
With gentility.
Let the awareness
Of your presence
Instill gentleness
In my soul;
Gentleness towards myself too,
The broken mirror of your love.
Let my self-presence share
In your forgiving presence
To my fragile life.

Coming Closer to God

Throughout this book, we have seen that a closer relationship with God, cultivated by the prayer of presence, brings us closer to one another. "I give you a new commandment: love one another; just as I have loved you. . . . By this love, everyone will know that you are my disciples" (Jn. 13:34–35).

Many human commandments are impositions. Often they seem forbidding. They dry up life and love. They do not lift up mind and heart nor create warmth and intimacy. Jesus' new commandment, by contrast, is a source of togetherness and healing. The gift of his love makes us appear to one another as symbols of divine generosity. His love widens the heart; it opens up to people.

He himself asks us to love one another just as he has loved us. He has loved us as uniquely chosen by the Father; as created in and through the Divine Word in this space and time; as called forth by the Spirit to a unique mission in life. He has loved us to the end, giving his life for us. He embraced us in our sinfulness, our reluctance, our resistance.

The Lord wants our lives to be a radiation of his

love in the midst of humanity. Many today are stricken with the terror of isolation. They feel lost and forlorn in a loveless world. Eagerly they seek for remedies. New techniques of encounter and communication are invented almost daily. Such techniques are in vain if they do not lead us to the ground of our oneness: the love of God.

Often that love remains hidden in our broken lives. At times it comes to light. In a moment of generosity, we are clothed in his love. He invites us to believe in that love hidden in the weak ones, in those who are temperamental, in the sick, the suffering and the poor, in anxious and tense people, in our own confused and suffering lives. He wants us to meet in love each suffering person, those who seem fools and failures, those who cross us, who hold different values, who threaten us by alien attitudes.

The love of the Lord is not a gift to be buried but a light to shine for many. His love in us appeals to the best in the other; it says to him: "Please be yourself. Realize what God has given you."

Loving words are rooted in the silence of listening to the other. This silence may be the only way to speak when the other is estranged from himself, not knowing who he is, imitating the crowd. His life may be like a collection of dead wood where only a few buds of life remain.

It is the love of the Lord in us that may help him to uncover the buds of his own life, to burn the dead branches, and to provide nourishing soil for a new beginning. Love often forms others by not forming; it leads by not leading and advises by not advising. The loving Christian listens to the feelings of others. Because he shares God's love for all people, he can distance himself from his own feelings. Such detachment leads to relaxed flexibility.

Divine love leads to an ecumenism of the heart. It enables us to respect the good will of the other. Ecumenism of the heart prevents us from rejecting the world of the other. It makes us sensitive to any part of that world we can accept and assimilate into our own heart.

The heart of the Christian expands itself in this loving encounter with a variety of people, thoughts, feelings and attitudes. This ecumenism is a must for the Christian engaged in apostolic endeavors, for love is the bridge to the heart of the other. The loving Christian is experienced not as an insensitive force but as a fellow human being genuinely interested in the world of the other.

Divine love is a gentle readiness for respectful dialogue. For the loving Christian, it is easy to commune with others. He gives himself to them generously, but he is also ready to receive. Sometimes her greatest gift to the other is her receptivity to what the other can give to her. When he is receptive, he allows the other to grow in generosity.

Divine love makes us adept in the gentle play of giving and receiving. This trait alone makes it a rich experience to meet with a loving Christian. He lives this attitude in relation to God himself. She gives to the Lord her thoughts, feelings, and activities. He receives from him grace, illumination and inspiration. The life of the loving Christian is like a liturgy. It is a constant consecration in which her gift to God is divinized and becomes the gift of God to her.

Divine love fosters an evocative attitude. The loving Christian evokes in the other the unique openness he or she is called to by God. Meeting a loving Christian, a person feels less compelled to assume a front. He does not have to play the game of hide and seek. He can be what God allows him to be in a relaxed and easy manner. The mask of social hypocrisy drops off and one enjoys an encounter that is life-enhancing.

We can observe this evocative attitude most strikingly in the encounters of our Lord. His meeting with his disciples, with Mary Magdalene, with the woman at the well were marked by a love that evoked in others what God wanted them to be.

We may now understand why the Roman historian Minucius Felix characterized the early Christians of his time as people who "love each other without knowing each other." In his commentary on the life of St. John, St. Jerome tells us that John was asked by his fellow Christians why he kept repeating, "Children, love one another." His answer was, "Because this is the commandment of the Lord, and if we only follow it, it is enough."

The prayers in Book Two blend the inspiration of love with its incarnation in daily service. They reveal the self-giving quality of Christian love — a love marked by peaceful reconciliation, discretion, patience and empathy.

Christ carried his cross for us, but not instead of us. Each Christian is given his own share of the cross to carry, his own function to perform for the sake of building the Kingdom. Each of us is called to draw all things to reconciliation with Christ through the ordinary, everyday encounters and trials of life. No matter how small the field of action may seem to be, the Paschal Mystery can operate wherever there is a person ready to open him or herself to the pain and peace of this transformation.

Receptivity to grace is at the same time an active call to go out and grasp what life offers us — the opportunity to love God with our whole heart and soul and mind and our neighbor as ourselves. The prayers that follow are thus a reminder of our dependence at each moment on the never failing grace of God and an invitation to live Christian values in the modern world.

You Are My Homeland

You order all things graciously.
You are the mystery
Unfolding cosmos and humanity.
You are my homeland,
My most original ground.
Your Presence
Welds all things together.
You are the caring love
That carries me
Like mother earth
Does forest, flower, tree.
Outside you
The world is a wilderness,
The universe indifferent,
The earth a barren planet
And I a speck of dust.
Your Presence alone
Is lasting home;
You are the Beyond
In the midst of daily life,
The sacrament of everydayness:
Immersion in daily duty
As flowing from your hand
Is homecoming to you.

BOOK TWO

Prayers of Presence

Part One

Prayers by Adrian van Kaam

The ten prayers presented in Book One were all composed by Adrian van Kaam. His collection continues here.

ICON OF THE LIVING GOD

You are the friend
Who holds me tenderly
In the palm of your wounded hand.
You share my sadness
With moist eyes and gentle smile.
You grieve with me in my distress,
You share your life
Laid down and spent for me.
You split apart the shell
That shields my heart.
You bare the limpid treasure
At the bottom of my soul.
The icon of the living God,
The form of life
That has been mine
Before creation took its course.
You shed my wasted days
Like used up skin.
Embrace with me the suffering
That bearing fruit entails.
This barren branch in slow decay
Begins to bear again the grapes
That make a wine which stirs the heart,
The grace which makes divine.

Witness for Your Light

Thank you for the dawning of your Spirit
Who makes us witness to your light,
Heralds of your journey through humanity,
Proclaimers of a mystery
That transfigures earth invisibly
At its hidden core.
Let us not betray your mellow call
By coercion of an anxious soul.
The witness of appeal should be gracious and mild
Leaving space to surrender or resist
Your invitation to a luminous form of risen life.
Let our dwelling on this earth
Refract the soft light of your presence
Like a stained glass window filters
The radiance of the sun in countless color.
Make us light up uniquely the corner of the universe
Where we are placed in time and space
Like candles in a dark and empty hall,
Laying down our life little by little
In service of all who pass our way in history.
Let our love be strong and honest
Never a refuge from reality and suffering,
Not sentimental but impeccably right and fair,
So that not we, but you may rise in the heart
Of the multitudes in search of
A shepherd for their lives.

A LIVING MESSAGE
OF GENTLE LOVE

We thank you, Lord,
For your walking on this earth
As one of us.
You were a living message
Of gentle love.
May your love be the center
Around which our life forms itself
Like a shell around an oyster
With its priceless pearl.
Melt all resistance
When your love begins to fashion
Our heart and all its feeling.
Make us sense
The silent stream of love
That flows into humanity
From the mystery of the Trinity.

FLEETING SENSE OF YOUR ABIDING

Lord,
You want me to remain in you
As you remain in me.
You promise me fruitfulness
In my little niche in history.
Together we shall carry fruit abundantly
To delight the Father's eye.
He looks at both of us so tenderly.
He looks at you, He looks at me
And smiles upon our unity.
He shines forth in us
When I walk my daily path,
Alive in you, transformed in you
As a servant of humanity.
To keep in touch with you
Still and steadily,
Nourish me with your words,
Those shining bridges
That like rainbows
Harmonize my earthly doings
With the heaven of your presence.
Let them penetrate my busy mind,
My dried up soul, like fragrant oil.
If you grant me a fleeting sense
Of your abiding, let me not clutch at it greedily
But flow gently with the holy mystery
Of your appearance and departure
In my daily life.

THE WOMAN AT THE WELL

In the midst of daily chores
You struck her tired heart
With faith and holy expectation.
She was a simple woman
Small and forlorn on a country road
Yet you kindled in her, as in few others,
The yearning for the promised One,
The Anointed of God,
Who would mellow harsh humanity,
Gentling it like aromatic oil.
You gave her these new and marvelous tidings
Because she acknowledged her poverty of soul
Her need to be uplifted by your Love.
Arrogance died quickly in her.
Lord, I too feel small and forlorn
On the country road of an empty life.
Please, strike my tired heart,
Anoint me with your holy oil
So that my stubborn life may soften
And be permeated by your life, my Lord.

SONG FOR GOD

May I forget my water jar
And everything that weighs me down.
May I rise unencumbered in the sky
Like a carefree bird
Singing: Come and see
How the Lord has set me free,
How all creation is a melody,
A song for God,
A song still open-ended,
An unfinished symphony.
May I complete a little
The mysterious work of the Father
On planet earth
In my small corner of history.
May I share the divine completion of creation.
Let it be for me the very fact of life,
My daily nourishment.
Let me spend myself eagerly
As Jesus did.

Trusting in Your Presence

Wash away, O Living Waters, intolerance
   and indignation,
Dark specks disfiguring our life.
Let us no longer trudge through endless waste
   land,
Our heart heavy with bitterness and dumb
   rejection
Of those who erode our expectations,
Our dreams of an early eschaton.
Make the appeal of thirsty strangers music to our
   ears;
Let us share with them the moisture left in the
   water jar
You placed upon our weary back when you sent
   us out alone.

Keep us straight as an evergreen
When ravenous birds seek shelter in our branches.
Fill us with immense compassion
When arrogant people despise your gentleness
And deride your gift.
Hold our biting tongues, our furious gestures.
Let our incensed impatience not spoil the love
   story
Between the Eternal and the sinner who crosses
   our path.
Mitigate our anxious ardor, our spurious haste,
Our clever willfulness so eagerly outrunning your
   design
Make us faithful to the holy destiny they do not
   yet suspect.

Let us nestle trustingly in your presence,
As in a cradle of peace, a hidden paradise.
Permeate every cell and atom of our being
With your spirit of generosity.
Fill us with the joy of knowing
That the whole world rests wholly in your hands.

The Everlasting One in Whom We Share

Messenger of the Beyond,
Slow down this busy life
To taste the living waters
Flowing from your Spring of Love.
Open this shell a little with your wounded hand
That the ocean of eternity may rush into my dried
   up days.
Touch with tenderness the ruins of my life.
Light up the darkness of despair
That I may no longer balance fearfully
My water jar as if it were the globe itself.
For you are waiting along the freeway
On which my days speed hastily to their end.
Life will collapse, the jar will be broken:
You alone remain the everlasting one in whom we
   share.
Your love gives majesty to the meanest people;
Create space in me that I may not begrudge
Nor spoil the generosity you called me to.
Free me from strategic giving
Luring people into indebtedness,
Making them inmates of my big-heartedness.
Radiate your love in friendly eyes,
In tenderness of touch, in mellowness of voice
That all may feel lovable in spite of countless
   failings.

IF WE WOULD ONLY KNOW

If we would only know
How you call us in the outcry of abused creation,
The piercing wails of people in despair,
The whimperings of a little child.

If we would only know
That each appeal is a gift to us
A golden opportunity
To console pained members of your body.

If we would only know
How our soul is paralyzed by our plodding life
Full of chatter, idle dreams and warped desires
That drive us from your lovely sight.

If we would only know
How close you are to all of us,
It would thaw the chill that kills compassion,
The stubborn will that drives us
Like an angry ticking clock
Standing watch against an empty wall.

No longer would our heart be shallow, small
Logged with sentiments of an angry past
Like a silted harbor cut off from the clear sea
Of your rushing love.

STAYING WITH GRACE

Staying with grace is staying with you, my Lord.
The One who refreshes and makes new my day,
Who lessens my fascination with futile things
And awakens me to what only counts.
Keep touching me inwardly until the light of
    insight dawns.
Do not allow the flicker of light to die
Before it becomes a living flame consuming me.
Make me treasure the dawn that speaks inaudibly.
Make me cherish the moment of illumination,
Attune me to the tender beginnings of your
    inspiration.
Oasis in the wasteland of my life,
Still the noise of daily chatter
That I may hear anew the murmur of the living
    waters
Running through the universe.
Mellow me, refine my receptivity
That I may surrender graciously
To the blessings you bestow on me.
Let me hear your invitation whispered gently
Like the rains of spring.
Give me an angel's wing
To rise with you, Eternal Lord,
To light the shadows of this dying earth
With candles of compassion.

Fill My Emptiness with Longing

A void, a hollowness,
A child in agony
Cries out in me.
The wonder of your living water
May resurrect this hollow life.
Make it bloom again,
Make it bear fruit.
Fill my emptiness with longing
To lose myself in your abyss.
Longing may be pierced with pain,
But pain of love is sweet to bear
As long as there is faith and trust
That Brother Sun went into hiding
To reappear more radiantly
When night is gone.
Let your river streamline
My resistant life, dull the edges
Of this canyon, worn and ragged.
Mellow bitterness that mars the beauty
Meant for me from all eternity.
Let your river be a spring in me
Leaping up in dazzling splendor
The moment I awake in Everlasting Life.

MYSTERY OF LIVING WATER

Mystery of living water, renew, invigorate
A flimsy mind, a listless heart,
A feeble will, a scattered fancy
Before this idle life is swept away
Like a useless pebble
Into a sea of trivia.
Let the blinding light of the Infinite
Drive its golden wedge
Into the center of my being,
Let its shaft of love
Pierce my armor until I find
My hidden depth in the Eternal Word.
Fill my self with longing love.
Light a spark of wisdom
Amidst the shadows of my cleverness
Cut the countless threads
That keep me fastened to a fleeting earth.
Dig holes in my pretentious self
Calcified by willfulness and pride.
Make me aware
That the golden pellet of holy longing,
Though mixed with selfish sentiment,
Is a most precious and undeserving gift.
Mine only is its contamination.

CREATE A NEW HEART IN ME

Make my heart less earthbound, Lord,
My mind less drowned in small designs.
Let me run no longer after the seductive pipers
Of this small and narrow land
Of lust and arrogance.
Shake me loose from my rusty moorings
In worldly routines.
Shame me by the shallowness
Of a lost and empty life,
A sad succession of pursuits
Of earthly happiness.

Anxiously I hunted for fulfillment,
Evading me like a lark in flight.
When I thought I captured it,
The song had choked already
In its little throat.
Soon the graceful singer died.
I clutched only a bunch of feathers
In my grasping hand.

Grant the grace of sweet upheaval
To this dense and dreary life.
Let me meet you at the well of daily happenings
As once the woman did.
Create a new heart in me
That I may not return blindly
To all that used to be.

THE WINTER OF MY HEART

Thaw the tundra of my soul,
Uproot the weeds that choke your gift.
Till the soil, dig the furrows
In which your grace may softly sink
To weather the winter of my heart.
Do not allow your grace in me
To dwindle like seed
Choked off by weeds
That suffocate and drain its power.
Let me gather sweetness from your flowers
In the garden of my soul.
Let my ear remain attuned
To your silent voice of Love
O prophet of my destiny,
O infinite sea that carries me.
Let my life flow forth
From your prophetic call
In the stillpoint of my soul.

You Read My Heart

You read my heart, you see the secrets of my life,
My lostness in lust and little things, not harmonized
In loving worship of you alone, my Lord.
O let me be within your loving spotless Son
worshiper in spirit and in truth.
candle burning brightly for the Lord.
Turn my days into a joyful celebration
Of the Mystery that is my origin and end.
Unite me with you, high priest of humanity,
Alpha and Omega, beginning and end,
Firstborn of all creatures.
For you have chosen me
Before the foundation of the world,
You are the vibration of my soul
Make me a priest of the universe
Blending all creatures inwardly
Into a song of praise and adoration.
Let the radiance of your worship
Shine upon my daily doings.
Change the world before my inner eye
Into a revelation of your splendor,
Shining forth most brightly
The destiny of all that is.

USELESS SERVANT

Dignity you bestowed abundantly
On every human being.
Each one is a sanctuary
Hiding the mystery of a mission
That outshines in the eyes of angels
Mundane appearance and success.
It may be a retarded child,
A sick old woman, an outcast of society,
A foreigner who talks haltingly,
Each one is splendid as a lustrous opal,
Precious as gold in the sight of God.
Each one is redeemed by the blood of Jesus
And called by the Spirit
To play a role in the Kingdom
As will be known hereafter
When veils fall away
And the mystery of each life
Will stand revealed.
May I sing to people
About the mystery they deeply are,
About the Spirit in their plodding lives.
Already the fields are white
Ready for the harvest.
But few are the laborers
To gather your chosen ones
In the granary of the Spirit,
To separate the golden grain
Of their graced destiny
From the straw of attachment.

Lord, send me out into the fields
And when I have done all I could
Remind me kindly that I was only
A useless servant.

You Stand at the Door and Knock

You stand at the door
And knock, my Lord
Until I open up.
You want to eat with me
The bread of daily sorrow
And to break for me
The bread of your eternal love.
Let me open up with joy and eagerness
To receive you as my savior,
The savior of the world.
Let me recognize your knocking
When it comes through someone else
No matter how simple or sinful she may be.
Let me see beyond her charm or rudeness
The Spirit who may have chosen her
To light a candle in my life.
They may be called to carry
A message of the Paraclete for me.
He may be called
To form and fashion me
In the image of my Lord.
Let me never doubt
That the same spirit may use me too,
In spite of my own sinfulness,
To bring some love and light
To fellow sinners I may meet
More intimately.

We Believe in You

Daily we are put to death for your name,
Hated because we believe in you
And not in the city of humanity.
You made us into reluctant reminders
Of a Light that lays bare the ruthlessness of many.
You made us the butt of resentment,
Hesitant signs that are rejected,
Sources of unrest scorned and scoffed at.
Our dignity is debased and denied.
Beaten, we return to the city of humanity where
We yearn to be praised by people.
We resent being reminders and signs.
We flee into bland compromises,
Wishing the best of both cities.
But it cannot be . . .
You come back to us, O wounded Lord;
You whisper softly that we don't belong;
You withdraw us tenderly; you turn us again
Into victims of derision.
Today, if we hear your voice,
Let us not harden our hearts nor
Close the escape hatches of our soul.
Don't allow the bad angel to keep us
Captives of the city.

LET ME MOVE IN YOUR PRESENCE

Don't talk harshly to my soul
When I am wounded and small
For you are slow to anger, Lord,
Of kindness to all.
When I cry out in distress
Nurse me back to life
As gently as a nursing mother.
When I ponder things too sublime,
When I put my worth in self-perfection,
In calculation of accomplishment,
Free me from such willfulness
Through the gentle action of your love.
Holy is my life in your presence, Lord.
In you I rise daily
Like Venus from the sea,
Like Phoenix from the ashes.
You are the landscape of eternity
In which my life unfolds
Like a blade of grass after winter's cold.
The symphony of your Holy Will
Is a playful expression of Eternal Compassion
Flooding time and space.
Let me be a note in your symphony,
A tiny iron filing
Drawn to you, Magnet Divine.
Let me move in your presence
As a fish moves gently in water.
Let no event excite me unduly
Or shatter me beyond recall.
Let me live all things as passing incidents
Reflecting your light.

LORD, RESCUE US

Lord, rescue us
From despondency,
From an outlook,
Dismal, solemn and somber;
From prophets of doom,
Who grimly denounce
Graciousness and joy;
Moody and morose they are
Of dour disposition
Whose contagious affliction
Veils the eyes of many
From your joyful tidings.
Cure them from their self-hate,
Their despondent mood,
The anxious frown on their brow.
Help also those among us
Who under the guise of outgoingness
Hide a heavy heart;
Those who are torn to pieces
By sickly feelings of guilt
For the suffering of all humanity
And cannot believe truly in your Redemption;
Those who lie awake
Night after night
Helplessly exposed
To the lethal radiation
Of deeply buried rage
They do not know;
Those who are bewildered
By images of pain and torture

Destroying dear ones.
Touch their flushed forehead, Lord,
With your healing hand.
Relieve the burden
Of their heavy hearted
Holy life.
Halt the endless worries
That consume them needlessly.
Relieve us, dear Savior,
From the pent-up anger
That spoils
Our precious days.

WITH A CONTRITE HEART

Prevent me, Lord, from confounding
The mystery of your life in me
With willful self-mastery.
May my gentleness not be a facade;
May it flow forth from my inmost center
Where you reign supreme.
Save me from becoming
A proud paradigm
Of perfect self-control,
A worshiper
Of poise and self-possession.
Save me from the pressure
Of exalted ideals
That deny my humanness.
Let my soul not be maimed
By perverted gentility
Grant me the gift to pray
With a contrite heart
And to be saved daily
From the deception
Of pious fantasies.

GENTLE VISION

When I am the brunt of derision
Help me to lift my anger into your light.
I need a wider vision.
My sight is narrow,
My feelings twisted.
I cannot see the wider meaning
Of each event.
I hide in my shell
Like a frightened tortoise
Instead of placing my feelings
Against the horizon of the Eternal.
I pretend to be gentle
When I feel upset.
I live a lie
That twists and deforms my inner life.
However poor, it is this life you love.
Not perfect self-control,
Not phony sweetness,
Not fearful isolation
But an honest response
Of who I truly am.
Now I can hear your invitation
To lift these feelings into your light.
Now I can mellow my anxious strife
To reach perfection overnight.
Help me to relate what I feel
To your redeeming love.
Let me not become live with rage
But illumined with the gentle vision
That grants each event its rightful place.

In Your Sight

Lord, save me from the need
To be loved by all, to win acclaim
For a gentleness I don't possess.
Save me from a piety
That can't admit hostility
Smoldering in my soul
Let me mellow day by day
Following your gentle way.
When things unsettle me
Remind me they are allowed to be
By an Eternal Spring
From whom all things flow forth,
To whom they all return
After their allotted time.
Whittle away pious pretenses
To release my anger furiously
On deviants and evildoers
Forgetting I too am but a sinner
In your sight.

Lovely Spirit of The Lord

Praise you, Lord,
For your splendid promise
To send the Spirit,
Light of Light,
The gracious One
Whose radiation
Pierces like a laser beam
The wall we build
Around our hearts.
Lovely Spirit of the Lord
Dim the turmoil
Of frenzied words.
Clean away the arrogance
That pollutes the atmosphere
Of gentleness and love.
Temper our self assertion,
Soften our unbending stand,
Save us from deceptive dealings,
From policies of lust and pride.
Enlighten us, confused and caught
In argument and angry thought.

LET NO ANGER GROW IN ME

Lord, keep me aware
Of whom I feel angry with
That I may not punish the innocent.
Let no anger grow in me
Like a volcano ready to explode
At the slightest remark.
Before I bring my offer to your altar,
Let me be reconciled in my heart
With my brother who angered me.
Free me from the passion and compulsion
To crusade self-righteously
Against your wandering sheep,
Who lost their way.
Cleanse me from the pseudo-gentleness
Of high priests, pharisees, and vendors in the temple.
Let my anger not turn into self-hate
That I mistake for true humility,
Nor let me use your honor
As a pretense for blazing anger
Against my brethren.
O Christ, win this battle
Between you and the pharisee,
Who dwells also in my heart.

LET ME NOT SILENCE MY ALIVENESS

Let me not silence my aliveness
Nor withdraw my feelings from your grace;
Guard me against putting on
The death mask
Of a reigned gentility
Because I dare not own
My anger and aggression.
Let me not deaden all feelings
Nor deny my anger with you.
Let me not twist anger and aggression
Into pietistic anxiety
That poisons body and soul,
That fills me with a sense of doom
And the suffering of the damned.
Let me not accuse a fallen angel
Of a self-distortion
That is mine alone.

LAND OF LOVE

Thank you, Lord,
For consecrating our feelings
By showing anger,
By being sad, delighted, lonely.
Teach us how to rule aggression
Instead of being ruled by it.
May anger surge at the right time,
Come out in the right way,
As your anger did.
Grant us an eternal vision
In which passing insults lose their sting.
Anger they may arouse, but no longer
Rage and fury that insanely want to hurt.
Let angry feelings of rejection be tempered
By an awareness of being saved and cherished
By an Eternal Love.
Grant me the grace of respect for the slow pace of
     progress
Infinite Wisdom allowed in my life.
Don't let me push beyond borders
Fixed for me from eternity.
Let no hidden hostility
Disguise itself as zeal
For your Kingdom.
Inspire all people of noble purpose
To search for means that may diminish
The hostility that consumes humanity
Gentle Grace, transfigure a world of warriors
Into a land of love.

Praise to You, Lord Jesus

You ejected vendors
From your Father's house;
You assailed scribes and pharisees.
We adore your holy indignation
Nourished by love,
Love for the Holy One,
Love for the Kingdom,
Love for mortals
Burdened unbearably.
Gentleness was behind your indignation,
Infinite was your readiness
To turn anger into love.
Praise to you, Lord Jesus,
For assuming all of human nature,
Also anger and indignation;
For setting them on a new course,
The course of the Kingdom.
Let us not malign our feelings
But lift them into the light of the Spirit.
Instead of driving anger underground
Teach us to take its sting away.
May our lives no longer be poisoned
By anger we refuse to resolve.
Keep us relaxed and radiant in mind and body,
Wide open channels for your generosity;
Our health and gentleness no longer marred
By hidden feelings of hostility.

TENDER FLOWER OF HOLY PRESENCE

You are the One, the only One,
And yet I crave for countless things
With restless heart and mind,
Deluged by fierce desires
That know no bound.
Carry me beyond my idols;
Walk with me
In the softening light
Of simplicity of heart,
Of single-mindedness
From which flows forth my presence
Like fresh water from a spring.
Eternal Other, forgotten Source, mysterious Core,
Tend in me the tender flower
Of holy presence
That gently blooms
In the mild and even climate
Of equanimity.
Grant me a poor, gentle spirit,
Not lightly thrown into a frenzy
Of passing fads, obsessive hoarding,
or to a social fanaticism
That has no time
For the deeper hungers of the poor.

PRESENT TO MY DAILY TASK

Spirit of my Lord,
You want me to dwell in society
With a gentleness of heart
That keeps me open for your light.
Prevent me from being caught
In any social movement,
In any missionary enterprise,
No matter how beautiful and holy,
That would not be a movement
Meant for me from eternity.

Give me the wisdom and strength
To be wholly present to my daily task
Instead of being more present to undertakings
God did not will for me.
Grant me the humility
To accept the resources
God has allowed me.
Soften excessive forcefulness,
Tightness and anxious self-exertion.
Infuse me with a wisdom
That clarifies my motives,
That liberates me from the curse
Of enslavement to popular opinion.

Let the splendor of the works of others
Blind me not to the hidden splendor
Of my own endeavors.
Let me not abuse my self
Merely to please others
By taking on good works
They are engaged in.

Forgive me and heal me
When I abuse the general acclaim
For a great and holy enterprise
As an alibi to escape
My own calling.
Holy Spirit, teach me
To be your gentle follower
In all situations.

LET ME DWELL DAILY IN YOUR LOVE

Let me dwell daily in your love,
Let it give form to my unfolding.
Let me no longer be the lonely shepherd of my life.
Bring me home from the bracing highlands of the
    mind,
From the dead end streets in which I shiver in
    despair.
Shelter my soul tenderly when disappointment
    hems me in.
Do not allow my soul to grow ponderous and
    bleak,
Keep alive in me a glimmer of your joy,
Let no adversity defer my course,
Nor defeat my slow advance.
Put a spring in my step, a smile in my heart.
Let me spend this life lightheartedly.
Fill it with verve and inspiration.
Ploughing, we praise; sailing, we sing,
To land on the shore
That teems with your Presence.

The Mystery of Your Will

Lord, make the night of my life radiant
With the brightness of your birth.
Refresh my tired heart
With a new vision of your glory.
Make me share in your divinity,
You who share my humanity.
Be my master. Teach me
How to bear lightly my daily burden.
Be the lamp of my life,
O Lamb of God.
Teach me to yield peacefully
To the mystery of Your will.
Grant me the wisdom
To be firm without rigidity,
Forthright without harshness,
Forceful without ferocity.
Fill me with the gentleness of the child,
The meekness of the lamb.
Divine Child in me,
Pull me back
When I become too involved in this age,
Inscribe me in your book.
Let me share in your suffering and your glory.
Let me adore you forever
As the Lamb slain for our race
Alone worthy to receive
Glory, honor, praise.

Part Two

Prayers by Susan Muto

THE PRAYER OF INNER QUIET

Lord, lead me to silence
And the prayer of inner quiet
That I may follow your light to life eternal
The fullness and oneness I seek
Can never be found
Amidst the fragments of earthly life.
I seek instead the undivided splendor of your
    Kingdom.

I need silence to keep my life in perspective,
To hear of its passing and know that I am mortal
I need silence to heal me from the hurt of speech,
To hear in worldly sounds the Voice most pure.

I feel dispersed among dry leaves of endless
    prattle,
Lost in words that touch only surface meanings.
Silence plunges me into inner depths
Where night descends,
Handmaiden of your mystery.
In the night of sense deprivation
Your silence stills all words.
You are the measure against which I feel infinitely
    small
Your silence speaks to me of the mystery of being.
You spoke in eternal silence
The Word who was your Son.
The silence of loving attentiveness
Is the language you hear best.

Wisdom is to keep silent
And wait upon your Word.

What is prayer but to be quiet before you?
To still desire,
To give my petitioning tongue a rest.

In silence, with you as my Center,
We meet as friends.
Defenses drop,
There is nothing to hide,
No one to impress.
My secret self is known in the silence by you,
  Father,
Who from silence called me forth
And to whom, in silence, I shall one day return.

The Peace You Promise

Thank you, Lord, for looking
Upon us with love.
Thank you for twilight,
Deep darkness and dawn.
On this way you are
Our journey's beginning and end.
The sufferings we undergo
Are as nothing in comparison
To the peace you promise.
Let us become like children
Who run to their father in total trust
And see behind the sternest reprimand
A depth of untold love.

Your Own Presence in Me

If my soul is seeking you, O Lord,
How much more is it me you are seeking?
You give me grace
To resist mere worldly gain
And be your own disciple.
You give me faith
To rise above my weakness
And be with you in worship.
Of myself I merit no favor,
But you judge me infinitely worthwhile.
Freely, generously, graciously,
You awaken me from slumber
And never tire of calling.
You give me, amidst complexity,
The splendor of the simple,
The splendor of your word.
You let me read your message
Beneath all other meanings.
The goodness of your word
Is everywhere revealed —
And no where seen more clearly
Than in the One Beloved,
Your only Son, Our Lord.
Whatever worth I am
Is due to your own presence in me.
I am your belonging,
Called forth to serve
Until you call me home.

MIST SHROUDS YOUR MYSTERY

Lord, in your works you write your name.
I call you Wondrous, Holy, Beauty
Beyond all telling.
Though near in your works,
You are far in your being.
You hide yourself in a cloud,
A mist shrouds your mystery.
Only faith and love can guide me
On this way of unknowing.
Empty my heart of all that hinders
This dart of love from ascending to you
That I may glimpse your light,
Though it gleams only in darkness.

WITHOUT YOU,
I ACCOMPLISH NOTHING

Lord, you ask for my attention
While I grow more distracted.
Guide my actions and my life
Despite my human weakness.
When worldly ways take over,
Grant the grace of sweet return
To the road I want to follow.
Be patient when I falter.
Call me back before your altar
To the One I long to love.
Only when I listen
Can I learn to be submissive.
Otherwise selfish expectations
Mar my best intentions.
Seductive domination
Replaces self donation.
The trap of betrayal
Snaps before I know it.
Teach me, Lord, the lesson of kenosis.
Make my whole being
An embodiment of your love.
Without you, I accomplish nothing.
Only when your Spirit guides me,
Can I listen to your word,
Can I do your Father's will.

THE GRACE OF SHARING

Lord, you are the master
I am to obey,
Yours are the attitudes I must imbibe.

Thank you, for granting me the grace
Of sharing in your salvation
As the person I am.
To follow your way is to find
My true self.

Divine Master,
Show me my purpose
For being here.
Help me henceforth to tread
The path that leads to eternal life.
At the end of my earthly discipleship,
Grant that my final resting place
May be with you.

PILGRIM AT YOUR DOOR

Lord, let me not forget to feed on you
Lest my spirit become dry.
Dry and acrid like the desert sand,
Dissatisfied and bored trying to fulfill
My limited human will
Instead of soaring free
To follow without fear
The way of union you decreed for me.
Grant me the grace to withdraw periodically.
Clear my inner eyes of worldly dust
That I may see your radiant beauty everywhere.
In you all things flow as from a tranquil source.
Let me find my place in this most holy plan,
The place where I belong.
Let me live the promise of your peace
In my soul, in this land.
Plant these words like seeds within my soul.
Let them sprout like spring blooms
Fed by rain and sun.
Should I fail to feed on you,
Nourish me still with generous grace.
Let the seeds of good intention grow.
Come to my aid, for I am weak
Without your help, given repeatedly,
I cannot begin my homeward trek
Nor hope to arrive, a pilgrim,
At your door.

YOU LISTEN TO LOVE

Lord, love must embrace my time and place.
Thanks is such a small word
To express what I feel
About the love that lifts my heart to yours,
That opens your heart to mine.
Love is the way along which we are sure
To reach you,
For when all else fails you listen to love.
Its cry awakens you
In the darkest of nights
And you leap to the side of the soul
Who beseeches.
The broken heart you do not shame.
The humble heart you do not scorn.
Such is the way we come to you,
Broken and humble hearted,
And "My Love" is the greeting
We receive.

To Wait Upon Your Word

Lord, since you know me better than I know myself,
Show me the way to be at one with you.
Grant me the grace to wait upon your word
That I may love and serve you throughout all my days.
Give me patience when life fails to go my way
To wait upon the message you are trying to convey.
Teach me to be grateful for the gifts you give each day
That I may glimpse, if only momentarily,
The home you have prepared for me,
The place of peace awaiting me,
Not here but in eternity.

WE LOVE YOUR NAME

Lord, for your word we give thanks.
For letting us listen and gain enlightenment,
We praise your wisdom.
For teaching us that you alone are worthy
Of ceaseless adoration,
We love your name.
We sing it aloud until it seeps
Into the depths of our heart
And places us in silent communion
With your spirit in time and eternity.

To Wait Upon Your Will

Truly your ways, my God, are beyond what I can
    know.
From reason's view, everything seems reversed.
Your seeming distance is true nearness,
The prayer I find so poor,
Is the one you find most pleasing.
Reason leads me far,
But faith alone can cross the last abyss.
Let me lay before your altar
My weakness and my trust.
Teach me to wait upon your will
While being where I am.
Let me give you a free hand
To guide me where you must.
Lead me through this night
To a union that transcends all knowing.
Let me love you for yourself alone.
Then I shall be ready to go home,
Attentive to you for your sake and not my own.

To Soar Homeward with Ease

Lord, awaken me from the sleep of desire
That makes me oblivious to my heart's longing.
Lift the illusion that hides the truth
That giving up self is really gaining.
Allow my soul to soar homeward with ease.
Freed from entanglements of mere worldly concern.

Strengthen me, Lord, for the mighty task
Of removing obstacles that block your grace.
Lead my soul into a silence so deep
That only your voice reaches my ears.
Gather my wounded being to yourself
By detaching my soul from earthly desires
That tend to exclude remembrance of you.

In this lifelong endeavor to diminish desire
Help me endure the dryness I feel
As I follow you to desert places,
Refresh me with your endless graces.
The night is dark, the journey long,
But with your mercy lead me on.

A CHANNEL OF YOUR MERCY

Lord, you love my poor, imperfect self.
You let me live
According to the gifts and limits you have given.
You free me from the pressure of perfecting
An impossible ideal.
In your mercy you demand of me
No more than I can bear.
By your free gift of forgiveness
You relieve the gravity of sin
If I repent sincerely.
You ask me to become
A channel of your mercy
That I may share with others
The forgiveness shown to me.
Free me from deceptive projects
That boast of self redemption.
Purify my heart of foolish pride
And the need for constant consolation.
Grant me the grace to carry your cross
Place me on the path I am to follow
Freed from sin and sheltered
By your forgiving Spirit.

WHY DO I DOUBT YOUR PRESENCE

How easily I shun the darkness, Lord,
Forgetting you are there,
I fear the silent desert
And run from the arid night.
Why do I doubt your presence
In time of desolation?
Why do I doubt the blessing
You grant amidst affliction?
Remind me when I cannot see
In suffering you are near.
Let me welcome darkness
As much as morning light.
Teach me, Lord, to thank you
Whatever cross you send,
Though following you means
Forsaking worldly consolation
Keep me faithful to your word.
In sorrow let me bless you.
In joy exclaim my praise.

TURN MY STEPS TOWARD HOME

My Lord,
Show me the way you have chosen
That I may follow.
Let me be one in spirit
With those whose steps
You have already led.
They left me the message of your way.
Let me hearken to their words,
Let their example soften
Any hardness in my heart
That I may see the way and follow.
Let me read in a spirit of docility
That I may dwell patiently
In the darkness of not understanding
Until your spirit gives me light.
Your light alone can illumine my darkness.
Let me read with an innocent eye,
Hear with a trusting ear,
That your words may touch my life
And transform it wholly.
Lead me, Lord,
From the tangled forest of duplicity
To the path of simplicity.
Calm my disquiet with your own stillness.
Lift the clouds of egoism from my eyes
Lest blinded by pride I lose the way.
Witness my trying, Lord,
And when I weary,
Take my hand
Whisper direction to my heart
Turn my steps toward home.

YES TO THE FATHER

Father,
Your love sustains me
At each turn of the road.
Gently and lovingly,
You awaken my soul.
You await my turning
And forgive my weakness.
You never forget
The likeness between us.

The most common acts
Of breathing and eating,
Speaking and praying,
Caring and teaching,
Become invitations for inner awakening.
For seeing, though darkly,
Your outpouring of graces.

Total surrender to your holy will
Frees me from worry
And lets me grow still.
In these many faces
I see that Most Dear,
In these many voices,
Only yours do I hear.

Make me mindful of what Christ would do,
How he would respond on each occasion.
What care and compassion would he manifest?
How can he become the source of my yes?

Yes to the Father,
Yes to the Son,
Yes to the Spirit,
To all Three in One.

This yes is the imprint you have made on my soul,
The flame of love that burns deeply within,
The yes that makes possible the no to sin.
No to the old me
Gives way to the new,
Empty of pride, ready for you.

Another Fine Book from Resurrection Press

THE HEALING OF THE RELIGIOUS LIFE

Robert Faricy, S.J.,
and
Scholastica Blackborow

Foreword by George Maloney, S.J.

This book is meant neither for those religious who are completely satisfied with the way the religious life is going, nor for the complacent; nor is it for those who have lost all hope. It is for those religious who know that the Lord is faithful to his promises, that the Lord does not want their religious institutes simply to go into oblivion . . . that he wants to guide us to new and better things for the religious life and for religious.

> *"The Healing of the Religious Life* is a book of hope — hope for the apparently dwindling and dying religious congregations of the Western Church. Sister Scholastica and Father Faricy show us how to shift the basis of our attempts at renewal from the interminably revolving cycle of discussion and from the forests of paper in which we feebly hope to the original source of each of our congregations — the breath of the Holy Spirit, breathing where it will. Let us lift our faces to that wind, to that gale which alone can sweep us into the future he is designing."
> LUCY ROONEY, S.N.D. DE N.

> *"This work is full of hope and realistic optimism held out to modern religious and to any Christian pondering the future of a dedicated life in a religious community."*
> FROM THE FOREWORD BY GEORGE MALONEY

ISBN 1-878718-02-9   80 pp. $6.95

Published by Resurrection Press

Discovering Your Light *Margaret O'Brien*	$6.95
The Gift of the Dove *Joan M. Jones, PCPA*	$3.95
Healing through the Mass *Robert DeGrandis, SSJ*	$7.95
His Healing Touch *Michael Buckley*	$7.95
Of Life and Love *James P. Lisante*	$5.95
A Celebration of Life *Anthony Padovano*	$7.95
Miracle in the Marketplace *Henry Libersat*	$5.95
Give Them Shelter *Michael Moran*	$6.95
Heart Business *Dolores Torrell*	$6.95
A Path to Hope *John Dillon*	$5.95
The Healing of the Religious Life *Faricy/Blackborow*	$6.95
Transformed by Love *Margaret Magdalen, CSMV*	$5.95
RVC Liturgical Series: Our Liturgy	$4.25
The Great Seasons	$3.95
The Liturgy of the Hours	$3.95
The Lector's Ministry	$3.95
Behold the Man *Judy Marley, SFO*	$3.50
I Shall Be Raised Up	$2.25
From the Weaver's Loom *Donald Hanson*	$7.95
In the Power of the Spirit *Kevin Ranaghan*	$6.95
Young People and . . . You Know What *O'Malley*	$3.50
Lights in the Darkness *Ave Clark, O.P.*	$8.95

Spirit-Life Audiocassette Collection

Witnessing to Gospel Values *Paul Surlis*	$6.95
Celebrating the Vision of Vatican II *Michael Himes*	$6.95
Hail Virgin Mother *Robert Lauder*	$6.95
Praying on Your Feet *Robert Lauder*	$6.95
Annulment: Healing-Hope-New Life *Thomas Molloy*	$6.95
Life After Divorce *Tom Hartman*	$6.95
Divided Loyalties *Anthony Padovano*	$6.95
Path to Hope *John Dillon*	$6.95
Thank You Lord! *McGuire/DeAngelis*	$8.95

Resurrection Press books and cassettes are available in your local religious bookstore. If you want to be on our mailing list for our up-to-date announcements, please write or phone:

Resurrection Press
P.O. Box 248, Williston Park, NY 11596
1-800-89 BOOKS